Beyond
Words

Also by John Humphrys

Lost for Words

The Great Food Gamble

Devil's Advocate

Beyond Words

JOHN HUMPHRYS

How Language
Reveals the Way
We Live Now

HODDER &
STOUGHTON

First published in Great Britain in 2006 by Hodder & Stoughton
A division of Hodder Headline

The right of John Humphrys to be identified as the Author
of the Work has been asserted by him in accordance with
the Copyright, Designs and Patents Act 1988.

A Hodder & Stoughton Book

1

A CIP catalogue record for this title is available from the British Library

ISBN 978 0 340 92375 7
Export ISBN 978 0340 92419 8

Cartoon on page ix © by John the Brush

Typeset in Sabon by Hewer Text UK Ltd, Edinburgh
Printed and bound by Clays Ltd, St Ives plc

Hodder Headline's policy is to use papers that are natural, renewable
and recyclable products and made from wood grown in sustainable
forests. The logging and manufacturing processes are expected to
conform to the environmental regulations of the country of origin.

Hodder & Stoughton Ltd
A division of Hodder Headline
338 Euston Road
London NW1 3BH

To my son Owen, who has learned to read since I began writing about English. So far . . . so good.

Acknowledgements

There would be no book without the help of many people. I am grateful to friends and colleagues who have shared their thoughts and frustrations. Among them are Philip Booth, Kevin Cecil, David Cox, John Dwyer, Charlotte Eilenberg, David Jordan, Dilip Lakhani, Theresa Marteau, Iain McGilchrist, Annie McManus, Helen Mountfield, John Smyth and Tony Travers.

Luigi Bonomi has done what all literary agents must do: offered praise even when it's not justified. Rowena Webb, my editor, can indicate disapproval with the merest pause or drawn-out 'yee . . . ss'. Also essential. And Hazel Orme has saved me from myself more often than I care to remember.

Above all, my thanks to the readers of *Lost for Words* who inspired me to write this book and who gave me so much wonderful material that I could write another dozen. But I promise I won't.

John Wakefield

John's name should have equal billing on the cover of this book. I could not – would not – have done it without him. What's truly re-markable is that this is the third book on which we have collaborated and we remain friends.

Contents

What Have I Started?

If I have learned anything in more than forty years of broadcasting it is that it's almost always a mistake to predict the way the audience will react. After a particularly lively interview on *Today* you might well walk out of the studio confidently expecting the plaudits of the nation for having exposed a politician's mendacity and single-handedly rescued the democratic process. Then you see the emails from those listeners who think you are an arrogant prat who could possibly have added a smidgeon to the sum of human knowledge if only you'd kept your trap shut for more than a few seconds during the interview. It is bad for the ego but probably good for the soul.

There are one or two certainties on *Today*. You know that a story about cruelty to animals will always get a bigger reaction than one about cruelty to children. You know certain subjects will stir great passion in the breasts of a certain section of Radio 4 listeners: 'elf 'n' safety rules; political correctness gone mad; anything about the Union Jack and, of course, anything about the English language.

Lost for Words was my first and, I thought, my last

book on English. I hoped it would stir things up a bit (though I was mildly surprised to be described on the Internet as a 'pendant') and indeed that was one of the reasons I wrote it. Don't believe journalists who tell you that they are interested only in informing the debate. They want to be talked about as well – or at least have their work talked about. What I was un-prepared for was how big a reaction there would be from readers and how it would be expressed.

The book was a cry from the heart of an ageing hack who has made his living using words. It was a protest against the cavalier approach we have taken to teaching children English over the past few decades and a lament at the way our language is mangled and manipulated by those who should know better. The response to it has been extraordinary and hugely encouraging – and that is partly what prompted this book and what the first couple of chapters are about.

But there was another motive. Language is more than a tool for expressing ourselves. It acts as a mirror to our world, reflecting back to us the way we live. Our choice of language and the new words we create reveal an enormous amount about how we lead our lives today and how society is changing. And that is what this book looks at.

In *Lost for Words* I was not saying that language should never change (because of course it always does) but that grammar matters. One of the daftest things we ever did in our schools was to stop teaching it to children. Academics who should have known better came up with the absurd notion that rules somehow confined children, restricted their imagination. I argued that the opposite is true. Understanding the basic workings of grammar – even if you don't observe all the rules to the letter – can liberate. If you don't know how to construct a sentence, how can you express yourself?

To judge by my readers' letters, I was pushing at an open door. Some of them came, as you would expect, from what is unkindly called the Green Ink Brigade (GIB). The GIB get a bad press mostly, I suppose, because of their predictability. Some really do use green ink and write in the margins of the letter when they have filled the page. Some even scribble a few lines on the back of the envelope after they've sealed it. Some clearly believe they are the only people on the planet capable of spotting a noun used as a verb or a dangling participle. Some are, quite frankly, a bit barmy.

Even so, I am a passionate defender of the GIB – just as I am a passionate defender of Brian Haw and people like him. Mr Haw is the man who made such a mess of Parliament Square by protesting about Iraq. He set up a ramshackle camp and managed to stay there for five years until the police came and evicted him. But it took a new Act of Parliament to do it. He, too, may be slightly bonkers. He may even be wrong. That's not the point. If someone believes in something it's good that they say so – just so long as they don't hurt anyone else in the process.

The GIB hurt no one. Indeed, they boost the profits of the Royal Mail. They may exaggerate occasionally (I need a little more persuasion before I shall accept that ending a sentence with a preposition is the root cause of moral decay in this country) but their hearts and their heads are usually in the right place. So, let us salute the GIB for their eccentricity and their unflagging energy – though an author's life would be a little easier if they forsook their scratchy pens for a word-processor or even a typewriter.

Many people saw the book as an opportunity to share their 'pet hates'. The posher sent me their '*bêtes noires*'. The not-as-posh-as-they-think-they-are offered me '*bêtes noirs*', or maybe they thought such horrors could not possibly be feminine. My office became a menagerie of deformed and repellent creatures. We had become a nation of 'stores' not 'shops'. 'Drives' had become 'driveways'; 'windows' are now 'window areas'. There were no longer 'warehouses', just 'distribution centres'. You could no longer buy a blouse, only a 'top'. Small children routinely talk of their butts rather than their bottoms. Nothing was 'more than' something else, it was now 'in excess of'. Estate agents were blamed for that, as they are for so much else. And, to the horror of many, none of this was going to change 'any time soon'.

I began to feel I was at the centre of a web of

vigilantes who are forever on the look-out for some verbal-delinquency or other that has to be reported back to HQ. So I was the first to be informed when *The Times* printed a headline saying:

The Slowdown in the Housing Market is Gaining Speed

And when a farmer in the Lake District received a communication from the Department of the Environment talking about

the Sheep National Envelope

it was instantly put into a real one and sent to me. I was invited to squirm that a BBC newsreader had been heard to say:

Known offenders are being fed into a computer.

One long-suffering commuter shared my bafflement at trains being terminated and doors being alarmed. His own train was delayed, according to the announcer, because it hadn't yet 'platformed'. Someone else invited me to unmask the young MP Ed Balls, close buddy of Gordon Brown. How, the writer wondered, could he possibly be the rising hope of those stern and unbending Brownites if he could offer this comment on the notion of Britishness?

The danger with Remembrance Day is it becomes a purely backward-looking event.

Another wanted me to share his disdain for the Liberal Democrat leader, Sir Menzies Campbell, for having said in an interview during the leadership election campaign:

There is no silver bullet on carbon emissions.

'Is there a silver bullet to deal with *any* political problem?' my correspondent scoffed. 'They might as well say they "can't wave a magic wand" . . . which of course the idiots do say, all the time!'

The language of official bodies continues to get up the noses of lots of people, especially when it involves spending our money. One letter-writer was very upset that the Metropolitan Police had spent a small fortune changing its logo (think of all the stationery and signboards that would have to be redone) from 'Working for a Safer London' to 'Working Together for a Safer London'.

Another was exercised by the reported proposal (still 'out for consultation') that traffic wardens should be renamed 'civil enforcement officers'. Apparently these new beings would be given greater discretion, including imposing variable fines. Presumably this would mean you wouldn't have to remortgage the house for getting back to the meter five minutes too late although you would if you were a 'persistent offender'. But it was the change of name that really rankled:

Can you imagine ANYONE EVER storming into the living room, face purple with anger, and screaming: 'That f***ing civil enforcement officer has just given me a ticket!'

There's no getting round the fact that there is a whiff of sado-masochism among those of us offended by poor language. One woman wrote to me: 'I thought you would hate this so I had to send it to you!' What so upset her was a letter from a company that organises conferences:

> We have the capacity next year to enable you, if you wish, the opportunity to meet with these delegates within your meeting schedule. Obviously if you didn't want to meet with them we will offer you the facility to negative preference them individually.

Technical jargon goes marching on, crushing all before it. In the IT business they use 'legacy' when they mean 'old' (probably best not to ask why) and this is how a company that sells barcode-readers described one of their *very* old systems:

> A legacy narrowband wireless system that had served its purpose over 10 years but had gone end of life.

Isn't 'gone end of life' so much more evocative than 'obsolete'?

The Americanisation of English walks hand in hand with jargon:

> UK consumer goods manufacturers have gotten used to operating in this highly competitive market . . .

You might expect that in the *Wall Street Journal* or the *New York Times* but, no, it was the work of the Economist Intelligence Unit in a report sponsored by the German software firm SAP. Readers have noted the growing preference of European companies for so-called 'international English' over the real thing. Instead of discussions there are 'brain dumps' during which 'key learnings' may or may not be divulged. Recruits may be asked what they have in their 'skills basket', to which the response will probably be 'All righty!' A Swedish-owned company issued a press release from its London office about a collaboration with British Aerospace aimed entirely at the UK media but written in American English. They seemed surprised when this was pointed out to them.

And speaking of PR releases, a friend sent me this cheery greeting from a senior PR executive:

> Hope you are well and thank the lord for the rest-bite in the weather . . .

Businessmen have their own glorious way with words. Richard Lapthorne, chairman of Cable & Wireless, tried to defend a bonus package he wants to introduce for senior management. They'd get £220 million worth. He admitted the scheme was 'a bit idiosyncratic' but described it as a 'tool kit' [huh?] designed to introduce the sort of performance-related pay seen in the venture-capital industry. He said: 'It's not about instant returns. We don't get turned on *per se* by money.' Quite so. When last heard of, C&W was planning to cut three thousand jobs in the UK.

Even words and phrases that have long settled into our way of speaking still bring some people out in a rash of indignation. Sex, as ever, is a problem. Apparently it's quite absurd to say you want to 'sleep with' someone since the phrase refers only to the before and after and skirts the object of the exercise. And when it comes to the main event, my vigilantes are concerned with language again. Why do we talk of 'having' sex when it's the 'doing' that counts? And it's ridiculous to talk about 'going out' with someone when the whole point is to stay in – and not to fall asleep, either.

You begin to think you have found yourself in bed with lovers of lost causes. They never give up:

Billion. Yankspeak for 10^9 when it should be 10^{12}. The previous European term for *one-thousand-times-one-million* was 'milliard'; and I can't see why something with nine zeros has 'bi-' in its name.

Neither can I, but I don't know quite what I'm supposed to do about it. People are obviously looking for leaders:

Could you attempt to get the word 'fantastic' made illegal? One TV host uses it every other sentence and I'm sure gets paid enough to have a vocabulary.

Broadcasters are in the cross-hairs of many of my vigilantes – and quite right too. Weather forecasters probably get more flak than most, which is a shame because in my experience they tend to be very nice people. But there can be no pity in this business and a crime is a crime. Verbosity is regarded as an indictable offence:

They always say 'during the course of the morning' instead of simply 'during' and 'more in the way of sunshine/cloud' when they mean 'sunnier or 'cloudier'. 'More in the way of sunshine' must mean 'cloudier' to foreigners.

Nor does it help when they add that more in the way of sunshine will be 'on offer'. Has Tesco now cornered the market in fine weather too? The cartoonist John Smyth is baffled by 'sharp showers'. He says he asked what it meant but the man at the BBC didn't know. Since then, he says, the virus has spread and we now have:

The weather may become sharper.

He fears that sharp showers will come to haunt him like 'cold snap' does. But Mr Smyth – a self-confessed 'cheery soul' – is one of the many whose greatest loathing is for unnecessary words. When he went to buy a DVD the girl in the shop said she would 'pre-order' it for him. He told her he'd be perfectly happy for her simply to order it but she looked baffled. Nor does Mr Smyth approve of what he calls 'super-cool inversions'. Here's a flavour:

Team Britain
Travel Ireland
Squash Welling [It used to be called Welling Squash
    Club]

There are many, many more and all equally baffling. And what about this word:

worsenment

Someone told me he'd seen it in *The Guardian* – which turned out to be true. It was in the context of train delays: a 'worsenment' of services. *The Guardian* poked fun at it (quite right too) and claimed it didn't exist. But that was wrong. It does. Apparently it's the antonym of 'betterment'.

But let me not give the impression that all my correspondents were on my side. If only. I have been suffering a severe attack of the 'physician heal thyself' variety:

On page 84 you have committed a monstrosity in writing 'marginally less ridiculous'. Permit me to quote from Gowers . . . 'in recent years *marginal* has come to be increasingly used to mean no more than *small*. This misuse has now reached the status of an epidemic and every writer should make a habit of crossing out *marginal* as soon as he has written it . . .'

Quite so. I was a bit slapdash with some of my prepositions too. I'd written that my old friend, Rod Liddle, 'was fired from the BBC for writing rude things'.

The first reaction is, how did they do that? By cannon? Where did he land? Was he hurt? Surely it should be fired BY.

Mea culpa again. I'd also committed the solecism of writing about 'decent public schools' as though there could be such a thing as an indecent one. According to one reader I 'betrayed my provenance' by suggesting (slightly tongue in cheek) that 'cuppa' should be included in the *Oxford English Dictionary*. Another pointed out that it already is.

It's an intriguing thing, this business of what's right and what's wrong. I have always hated 'meet with' or, even worse, 'meet up with' and assumed it to be one of our less welcome American imports. More fool me for not reading my Kipling properly. After all, he tells us that when we 'meet with' triumph and disaster we should treat the two impostors just the same.

I was sniffy about 'outwith' but had to run up the

white flag after the umpteenth letter from angry Scots telling me it was not some modern version of guru-speak but a word used north of the border since long before I had uttered my first sentence.

'Test out' was another. I've always supposed the 'out' to be a redundant preposition. I reluctantly concede defeat to those who made clear that it is self-evidently a helpful adverb meaning 'thoroughly'.

I thought I was on safe ground when I scoffed at 'on a daily basis'. Surely 'daily' was more than adequate? Seemingly not. 'Day' is a noun and a noun may be turned only into an adjective and not into an adverb. So it turns out that it's wrong to say you swim daily and correct to say you do so on a daily basis. If we wanted a single word instead it would have to be 'dailyly'. But perhaps not.

Turning nouns into verbs is viewed as an even greater offence. You do not have to be a member of the GIB to wince at competitors in the Winter Olympics hoping they would 'medal'. By the time of the Commonwealth Games sports commentators were confident our national athletes would 'podium'.

In *Lost for Words* I'd confessed I was 'baffled' as to why the phrase 'wheelchair-bound' should be thought offensive while 'wheelchair-user' was fine. I wasn't alone. One helpful reader asked a disabled friend (not 'differently abled': one must hold on to something here) and here's what he said:

'I am wheelchair-bound only once or twice a year. I enjoy it very much but I'm a reasonable man and I do understand that my wife doesn't enjoy it as much as I do and it takes a great deal of setting up to get the knots just at the right tension. Now would you like to share with me one of your most intimate moments with your wife?'

Ambiguity, of course, is one of the sources of comedy as well as misunderstanding in language. I wasn't always sure whether I was being warned about genuine problems of usage or whether I was having my leg pulled. I was pretty sure that the person troubled by the phrase 'child psychiatrist' was not really worried about under-age practitioners. And even though the pendulum may be swinging back in favour of selecting children on ability, I was not persuaded that the sign 'Slow Children Crossing' was in itself discriminatory.

But you never can tell. Someone got very upset by my translating the ancient Greek advice about how to live life as 'nothing in excess'. How could I possibly believe there could be an excess of nothing? The only accurate way of using the word is King Lear's: nothing comes of nothing. I should have written 'Everything in moderation'.

I suppose that's right but where does it leave the advertising copywriter who came up with the catchy line 'Nothing acts faster than Anadin'? Perhaps he was actually trying to subvert the pharmaceutical company that made it. I once had a minor operation and the surgeon advised me not to take the painkillers offered to me afterwards. It was good advice. The pain was unpleasant for a day or two but then the endorphins took over. 'Nothing' really was more effective – and much cheaper.

One woman drew my attention to the ambiguity in the phrase 'family butcher'. She could see the funny side of it. Not so a friend of hers who had grown up in Germany in the thirties and much preferred the straightforward German word '*Fleischerei*'. What intrigued me was why anyone should want to attach the word 'family' to 'butcher' in the first place. Was it simply to soften the impact of the uncompromising and graphic word 'butcher'? Is the phrase just a vestige of the era of warm beer and midwives cycling through villages on bicycles when the patrons of butchers' shops were, indeed, almost exclusively families?

If it is, maybe we should now have butchers labelled according to their more diverse contemporary clientele. Should their shopfronts read 'One-Person-Household Butchers', and 'Co-habiting Butchers'? Maybe gay butchers would become 'Pink Butchers', catering specifically to those who like their meat rare. Not that it matters. The way the supermarkets are taking over, there will be no butchers left soon anyway – except for the posh shops catering to only the most well-heeled customers and, of course, the Organic Butchers. Presumably the inorganic ones are made from plastic.

What unites the GIB, the vigilantes and the less militant readers is that we should give a hard time to all those (usually people trying to sell us things) who use language that is clearly intended to mislead.

I am partial to the occasional bag of crisps. The brand I buy claims to be 'handmade'. How? They sell tons of the things in shops across the land. Am I really supposed to believe that vast teams of workers spend their lives making crisps by hand? Don't they have *any* machines in their factories? And how do you 'hand make' a crisp anyway? A piece of pottery or a nice hand-knitted sweater maybe, but a crisp?

Like most people, I have failed to penetrate the mystery of hedge funds. The one thing I do know is that 'hedging' your bets is a way of reducing risk. Yet hedge funds are among the riskiest of investments on the market.

On one level it is reassuring to know that so many people share one's irritation and occasional amusement at this sort of thing. On another, it's slightly alarming. If my correspondence is a reliable guide, people out there are being driven to distraction by it. What can be said to the lady who complains that her life is made a misery by the contradiction in the phrase 'I don't know, I'm sure'? Or to the person who wrote:

I writhe in frustration at: 'What did you say your name was?'

Well, yes, I take the point about names not changing, but one shouldn't get too tense about tense. On the other hand, because of the sheer madness of the following, I warmed to the woman who wrote this:

Having called into Tesco's one evening on my way home from a girlie lunch, I arrived at the check-out where a young man in his mid-20s began to cash-up my purchases. I interrupted my packing to give him some money and as he handed me the change he said, 'There you go.' I looked him in the eye and the following conversation ensued.

'What does that mean?'
'I dunno.'
'Why do you say it, then?'
'I dunno.'
'Well, that's very interesting. Here we are with speech enabling us to communicate thoughts and ideas, yet you say something to me not knowing what it means or why you say it.'

The young man looked at me with his mouth open. (By this time the girl at the next check-out was on her feet, straining to hear what was going on and nudging the girl next to her to also pay attention!)

At this point my reader thought of quoting Henry Ford, the maker of the Model T. He not only said you could have it in any colour so long as it was black, he also said running a business would be a cinch if it weren't for the customers. But she decided against that. Instead she told the hapless young man:

'I think you say that because you think saying "thank you" is demeaning.' As no thoughts or ideas were forthcoming I resumed my packing, squashing into the bag the last item as I barked, 'And you haven't said it yet.'

He managed a stuttered 'Thank you.'

The woman had the good grace to admit that in retrospect she felt a touch of sympathy for the target of her wrath:

'Poor young man! Whenever this episode surfaces I either scream with laughter or go hot and cold at my harshness.'

Quite so. But we shouldn't let embarrassment at our occasional excesses deter us from making a fuss about the mangling and manipulating of language. The campaign must go on. I take some comfort from the knowledge that I have more than the massed ranks of pedants on my side. I have the Goths too. Early in 2006 an article appeared in the *Sunday Times* head-lined:

Goth-rock Hero's Darkest Secret

It was by Robert Sandall and was about Ville Valo who (for those of you who may not know it) is 'the lead singer of the elegantly doom-laden Finnish band Him'. Mr Sandall wrote:

> An hour or so after Him finished their set at the Paradiso club in Amsterdam, Valo is back in the hotel bar studiously ignoring a gaggle of silently adoring female fans who have somehow managed to trace him here. This tiny fraction of the girl-led mob milling around the venue after the show ended are now disappointedly cradling drinks while their hero presides over an all-male coterie comprising his bandmates, manager and an English journalist (me).
>
> But the person who has helped him most recently in his battle with words and meanings is – no kidding – John Humphrys, the presenter of Radio 4's *Today* programme. 'I just finished his book *Lost for Words*,' says Valo. 'I love people who are passionate about their language and appreciate the history of it.'

I can't tell you how hurtful the 'no kidding' was.

CHAPTER ONE
Making Sense of Making Sense

There is one thing we have in common. All of us. You
and I and the slightly menacing young hoodie hanging
around on the street corner. We all care about language. Your concern may be different from the young
hoodie's. You might contemplate climbing Everest
naked before splitting an infinitive. He cares just as
passionately about using language that proves his
street cred. We each need to take care. His language
is changing almost every day. A word that was a
compliment yesterday may be an insult tomorrow.
Ours is changing too – more slowly, but just as surely.

The point of this book is to look at what our
changing use of language reveals about the way we
live now. It is about our attitudes, about the way we
see things and how we are seen by others: in public
life; in politics and commerce; in advertising and
marketing; in broadcasting and journalism. Language
provides us with a revealing mirror on contemporary
life. But we will be able to recognise what it shows us
only if we know how words work and how they are
abused. Yet the prevailing wisdom about language
seems to be that 'anything goes'.

It's important to be clear about what should *not* worry us. I don't get at all agitated about the good-natured lad doing a dreary job on a supermarket check-out who tries to be amiable by passing meaningless remarks to a slightly batty customer. Nor does it worry me in the slightest that he may use an alien (to me) language when he's discussing the merits of one MP3 player against another. And he hardly needs to speak formally correct English when he's chatting up girls in a bar or talking about his football team with his friends.

He has his world and I have mine and we each speak our own kinds of English in them. But we also have a shared world where we need a dependable common language if we are all going to get by. And what matters is not so much how the lad on the check-out may use language in this shared world, but the attitude of so many academic experts to that common language.

As an interviewer, I spend my life asking experts questions for the very good reason that they know more than I do. The problem with a life spent in journalism is that you end up knowing a tiny bit about every subject under the sun but not a great deal about anything in particular. Like any halfway competent interviewer I can make a credible job of interviewing an expert for a few minutes on even the most arcane subject. Stretch that beyond five minutes and I start to flounder. But on this one issue – our common language

– I'm happy to mix it with the experts. That's because when they should be getting exercised and passionate they tend to relapse into a state of indifference. Their attitude to the condition of the very thing they have spent their lives studying amounts to little more than 'hey, whatever . . .'.

Professor David Crystal is the experts' expert, the *capo di tutti capi* of the linguistic Cosa Nostra. He has probably written more books on the English language than any other living soul: more than a hundred so far and he will almost certainly have written another in the time it takes me to finish this chapter. What Professor Crystal does not know about the structure and history of English is probably not worth knowing. He also writes brilliantly. Mere journalists like me are scarcely fit to hem the fabric of his academic robes. Yet he infuriates me.

Here's a small example. He does not think it much matters if we put apostrophes in the wrong place. So he would not, presumably, have given a fig if he'd read a press release entitled:

Lecturers Pay Dispute

that went on to talk about 'student's exam papers'.

I mention that one specifically because it happens to have been sent out by the office of Boris Johnson, the Shadow Minister for Higher Education. David Crystal selects the more common example of the greengrocer selling 'potato's'. He does not reach for his horsewhip;

he merely points out that in the eighteenth century it would have been perfectly acceptable. Indeed, he says, it is perfectly acceptable in the twenty-first century because there is no room for ambiguity. Everyone knows it must be a plural for the obvious reason that we know potatoes cannot possess things.

Well, that's true. But the great Keith Waterhouse, founder of the Association for the Abolition of the Aberrant Apostrophe, makes a different – and vitally important – point. Unless you get into the habit of being precise you'll be open to misunderstanding when something is capable of having two meanings. He once offered this example:

Prudential – were here to help you.

Sometimes an apostrophe can be a copywriter's saviour. But experts as eminent as David Crystal have no truck with the likes of Waterhouse and Lynne Truss – or, indeed, with me – when we write about the use of English. He compares us to car mechanics who have had no training but 'write repair manuals about language and expect other people to live by their recommendations'. He goes further:

In fact, the people who write manuals are more akin to doctors than mechanics, because they take the view that a great deal of language use is unhealthy, and that a large proportion of the population is linguistically sick without realising it. Having persuaded others that they are unwell, they then offer remedies in the form of usage tablets of their own devising. Talk or write like me, they say, and you will be well again. The word *doctor* was wrong: these are the equivalent of the nineteenth-century quacks.

So that's us told, then. It's an interesting notion that the only people qualified to write about the use of English are those who have been trained to do so. For a hack (or 'quack') like me to square up to David Crystal may well be a bit like a go-kart challenging a Ferrari, but there's no reason not to try.

Professor Crystal seems to believe that so long as we are intelligible we can be as cavalier as we like with the rules and conventions of language. What's more, he thinks those rules and conventions can take quite a battering before we lose the sense of what someone means. In the most narrow sense that's true. One reader demonstrated it by sending me a letter that included this:

Aoccdrnig to rscheearch at Cmabrigde Uinervtisy, it deson't mttaer in waht oredr the ltteers in a wrod are, the olny iprmoatnt tihng is taht the frist and lsat ltteer be in the rghit pclae. The rset can be a taotl mses and you can sittl raed it wouthit a porbelm. Tihs is bcuseae the huamn mnid deos not raed ervey lteter by istlef, but the wrod as a wlohe.
  Amzanig huh?

And, dammit, it's true. I did get the full meaning of what he had written in spite of the grotesque spelling. So does that prove we are making a fuss about nothing? No. Here's how the letter (which, by the way, came from a former head of English in a comprehensive school) continued:

> What is not made clear, of course, is that in order to decipher the jumble, your own mind has to have a semblance of order in the first place. This is exactly why we need rules and conventions. There has to be a common code of communication and this piece of research does in fact prove exactly the opposite of its hypothesis. Without a common code, it could not be understood.

In any case, the idea that intelligibility is all that matters is deeply suspect. Intelligibility itself is a slippery notion. When we hear something that's said in mangled language we may think we understand what's meant but we may be mistaken.

After Hurricane Katrina hit the Gulf coast of the United States an official from New Orleans said in a radio interview:

> The magnitude of this disaster is untenable.

People who heard it probably thought they knew what she meant. But what exactly did she mean?

The problem is that it doesn't make sense to say a magnitude is untenable. It could be that she meant the scale of the disaster was unbearable. She may have thought 'unbearable' was too personal and emotional a phrase for an official to use so resorted instead to 'untenable', which sounds more neutral, more 'official'. It is akin to the way many public figures avoid saying that something is 'wrong' (too loaded) and settle instead for saying that it's 'inappropriate'.

Or she may have been making the almost metaphysical point that the magnitude of the disaster was incomprehensible, impossible to get hold of.

Or perhaps this was just extreme shorthand. What she was saying was that the scale of the disaster was so great that Washington's slowness in getting to grips with it was becoming politically untenable.

Who knows? Probably most people would have thought she meant no more than 'Gee, it's awful!'

And that's the point. Mangled language may be intelligible but only when we settle for some lowest common denominator of meaning. If we're happy to let our common public language be used in this way, communication will be reduced to a narrow range of basic meanings. What we will understand (and all we will come to expect) from it is a rough, approximate meaning rather than anything precise or subtle.

That, of course, would be rather convenient for snake-oil salesmen, unscrupulous estate agents and (dare I say it?) even some politicians who might prefer not to be pinned down to anything too precise. But why should the rest of us settle for lowest-common-denominator communication when we have the great Voltaire on our side? He put it this way:

> Loss of your subjunctive is the loss of your civilisation!

A trifle over the top perhaps, but mere intelligibility is simply not good enough.

Bad language often buries meaning. A friend who does some work for a consortium of universities was presented with this proposition:

> The participants are increasingly identifying the need for radical change which weaves together renewed attention to a vision of citizenship for all, direct engagement with people using support and the major shift in culture required to ensure delivery prioritises person-centred support and connections to the wider community.

He had not the slightest idea what it meant – or, at least, he couldn't be bothered to work it out. If you make the effort you can just about discern a meaning, but why should we have to? Professor Crystal would say that if it's intelligible it's OK; I'd say that if it becomes so only through the sort of struggle that makes bashing your head against a wall seem pleasant, it isn't.

A vicar told me about his years as the chairman of his local residents' association. He was, as he put it, 'showered with bumph from the local council'. Most of it was written in extraordinary officialese. Not wishing to let them get away with it, he demanded simple translations even when he didn't really need them. For example, he had asked what was meant by 'low-profile landscape'. He was told it meant 'flat'. Well, of course it did, and of course he knew that, but he made a fuss about it for the best possible reason. If officials on your local council don't use the same language as you do, the impression comes across that they don't share your world and they don't want you to share theirs. Or, as the vicar put it:

> The danger is that bodies like governments and councils will get away with murder simply because they have wrapped up what they are doing in special language.

'Or careless language', he might have added. A woman whose father had recently died told me about the letter she received from a firm of solicitors:

> With regard to the estate of your diseased father . . .

It reminded me of the epitaph Spike Milligan said he wanted on his gravestone: 'I told you I was ill.' But it's funny only if it happens to someone else. You have to wonder what's going on when a firm of lawyers – the very profession whose use of language must be precise – can do something quite so idiotic and unthinking.

You wonder if they realise that a real, vulnerable human being is at the other end of their pathetic attempt at communication.

So, with great respect to Professor Crystal, intelligibility is not the only criterion by which our common language should be judged. It should also make us feel at home in a shared world and not alienated from those with whom we are supposed to be sharing it.

But there are good reasons to wonder whether, in the way we communicate with each other, we do still share a common world and, if so, how long we shall go on doing so. Some interesting new phrases are entering the language, which take us into a different world: 'digital native' and 'digital immigrant'. The immigrants are people like me, no longer in the first flush of youth, who have not so much embraced the digital age as accepted its inevitability and tried to learn as much as they need to cope. The natives probably learned to use a mouse before they could read a sentence and simply cannot imagine life without the ability to send text messages or join in conversations in cyberspace.

Some of them will speak a language that is incomprehensible to the other half of the population. Students and children at school will engage in 'wiki-thinking', which means exchanging ideas through digital networks. It derives from the Internet encyclopedia called Wikipedia, which has been built up not from the knowledge of individual academics and experts but the collective knowledge of thousands of contributors. Some of it is rubbish. Much of it will add to the sum of human knowledge.

Richard Woods wrote a thoughtful piece in the *Sunday Times* about the impact of this generational divide between the immigrants and the natives. I'm interested in its effect on language. Dr Anders Sandberg, who is researching cognitive enhancement at Oxford University, told Woods that anecdotal evidence suggests people are becoming more visual than verbal. He said some people are claiming that 'once computers gain good language understanding and we can speak to them, then reading and writing are going to seem cumbersome'.

That is an alarming prospect. Visual images are often more powerful than the same things described in words. I doubt that any of us will ever forget the pictures of the Twin Towers crashing to the ground. Photographs of a child starving to death or a mutilated body lying in the rubble arouse us to the heights of pity or anger.

But what the pictures cannot do is express the complexity that might help us understand why these terrible things are happening. Only words can do that. A world that depends more on images and dismisses reading and writing as 'cumbersome' will be a much cruder and probably an even more dangerous place. I hope I never see it.

Happily, it's not here yet. Until it is, language is what we'll continue to use to negotiate our way around our shared world – for better or worse. Let me give you an example of the worse. In the course of a year I get hundreds of requests for help from 'media study' students. I try to resist telling them that many (if not most) 'media' degrees are about as much practical use as a cat-flap on a submarine and I do what I can to help. But this particular email strained my courtesy to its limits. I reproduce it exactly as I received it:

Dear Mr Humpreys,

I am a 3rd year student of Politics and Communications at the University of Liverpool. I'm am currently writing my final year dissertation on the future of UK PSB. My specific research question is:

'Is the notion of universal public service broadcasting provision, institutionalized around traditional mainstream broadcasters, an obsolete one in the multi-channel media era?'

I was hoping you may be interested in offering a few comments for the 1st chapter which consider's whether UK broadcasting is seeing a return to 'the golden age' of television by way of programme variety and content. I am argueing that there is a return to that level of provision and that quality and range-while not perfect is getting better, particularly so across the BBC but is limited elsewhere, you may agree or disagree. As a senior broadcaster and vocal commentator on broadcasting issues, i feel you could offer some valuable general observations of the current broadcasting landscape on the topic of provision by PSB's – these would be of immense value to my dissertation if you could spare a couple of mins to share your thoughts. Of course i would happy to provide you with a couple of the final dissertation as a show of my appreciation.

Thankyou for your time,

I look forward to hearing from you,

Best wishes

I shall spare the young man's blushes by not printing his name but it raises a number of questions. The most obvious is how someone who is barely literate might seriously believe he has a career in a trade that requires him to write the odd sentence.

Another obvious one is how he has managed to get to the third year at university without being sent off on some sort of remedial course. It is a sad commentary on the state of English teaching in schools that most universities now offer such courses. The Oxford University Press has just published a new dictionary for students in response to lecturers' complaints that they're forced to waste time correcting basic errors of grammar. The dictionary's editor Catherine Soames says: 'Ideally it should have been learned at school but often it is not, so we are helping students redress the balance.'

The other question is how the young man made it to the third year without being advised to consider another course. I suppose the answer to that one is simple enough: universities need students to cover their costs and who cares if they waste three years of their young lives when they might be doing something to which they are better suited? Or maybe that's too cynical.

Or maybe it was *he* who didn't care. That may explain why he did not even bother to check how my name is spelled or pick up any of the howlers (I gave up counting when I got to twenty) in his email. Maybe he was listening to his iPod or chatting to his girlfriend as he typed it. Or maybe – and this is too depressing to contemplate – he simply didn't know. If that is the case, I suppose one must feel sorry for him.

Soon after I heard from the student, the Royal Literary Fund published a report about the state of literacy among British undergraduates. In 1999 the RLF had sent professional writers as RLF fellows into universities and colleges to help students with the basic skills of writing essays and the like. The report was a compilation of their accounts of what they had found. The biographer Hilary Spurling, the chairman of the scheme, wrote:

The individual accounts read like dispatches from a front line where students struggle to survive without basic training or equipment.

One of the recurrent themes of the report is the confusion, embarrassment and fear endured by students who find themselves confronted with written assignments they don't understand and can't begin to tackle. The inability to write, based on lack of preparation and practice, destroys young people's confidence.

'Anxiety is at the heart of many of the problems students experience with their writing,' reports one of our writers. 'Some of them have not been asked to write an essay or its equivalent for years, and few have ever been told how to do it in the first place.'

She concluded:

Learning to write is no longer a purely academic issue. It is a question of our social, economic and cultural future. What began as a private scheme devised primarily for the benefit of writers has exposed a public catastrophe.

I hope the RLF report was read very carefully indeed by all those academics and English 'experts' who say intelligibility is the only criterion and that grammar doesn't matter so long as we can understand what is being communicated. It's perfectly true that I understood (just about) what my emailing friend required of me, though it took a little more effort than it should have done. But that misses the point. All those people who have written to me about the value of what they regard as decent English cannot be dismissed as a bunch of cranks living in the past. They are not saying the language must never change, must always remain as they remember it in some mythical golden age. They know it must adapt to changing times as it always has. But they do not want to feel alienated in the public space that, at some time or another, we all occupy. They are entitled not to be offended by semi-literate rubbish.

And what of my student? I suppose he's well into his dissertation by now – but he's doing it without my help. Perhaps I should feel guilty. Maybe it's not his fault that he can't spell or use punctuation. Maybe his teachers let him down. Or maybe the teachers themselves were let down. I have had many letters over the years from teachers who say they themselves were never taught the basics. So why, to pursue this to the bitter end, were the failings of the teachers not spotted? We do, after all, have a system of inspection.

Ah, but that assumes the inspectors themselves were capable of spotting their failings. Allow me to introduce you to a little booklet produced by Ofsted, the body responsible for inspecting the nation's schools and trying to ensure that our children get a decent education. It is twenty-two pages long and entitled *Guide to Ofsted's House Style*. Among those who received it were the school inspectors. We all know about them. Most of us can recall at least one morning in school when the teacher was reduced to a nervous, stuttering wreck because a stranger had come into the classroom and had sat quietly at the back watching and listening. It was the dreaded inspector, the Grim Reaper himself, scourge of incompetent teachers throughout the land. These were the men (almost always men in those unenlightened times) who sat in judgement because they were the People Who Know Everything. Their word was law. Now even *they* are deemed to be in need of a little help when it comes to writing.

When I asked Ofsted about the guide, they told me it is to help people (including the school inspectors) write their reports 'in a clear and consistent style so that readers can readily understand their content'. Fair enough. Nobody's perfect. But let me give you a flavour of the content. Here's part of what it says about apostrophes. They are not to be used to indicate plurals but to . . .

> . . . indicate possession . . . Note the difference be-
> tween 'its' and 'it's'. The former is a possessive
> pronoun and does not take an apostrophe. The latter
> is the contraction of the words 'it is' or 'it has' and
> does take an apostrophe.

And here are some examples of apostrophe use that Professor Crystal presumably would think even Ofsted inspectors need not worry their little heads about:

> 'The children's books' (The children own the books.)
> 'The ladies' cloakroom' (The ladies use the cloakroom.)
> 'The women's singles tournament' (The tournament is played by the women.)

There is help, too, when it comes to confusion over when to use 'I' and when to use 'me' or 'myself'.

> Use 'I' if you are doing the action of the verb (for example, the speaking in 'I spoke to him'). Confusion can arise when there is more than one person doing the action ('Claire and I spoke to him') or having the action done to them ('He spoke to Claire and me'). If you are unsure which is correct try removing the extra person from the sentence. 'He spoke to I' is obviously wrong.

Who can argue with any of that? The great Fowler himself could not have put it better. It's just the sort of stuff I hope my little boy will be taught over the next few years. But that's the point. He is barely six years old. Shouldn't we assume that the people who run our schools inspection system already know all this? Ofsted insisted this was not aimed at teaching basic grammar to inspectors, oh dear me no. It was aimed at all Ofsted people and is intended, as its title suggests, to 'provide guidance about stylistic conventions . . . to help ensure all Ofsted and other publications or reports adhere to a clear and consistent style'. I was told this was similar to a newspaper's style guide and that, it seems, makes all the difference.

Well, I'm afraid it doesn't. Grammar is not style and style is not grammar. Style is about whether you capitalise certain words or indent paragraphs or use single or double quotation marks and a thousand other stylistic things. It is NOT about the basic rules of grammar. Yet it is those very rules that Ofsted seems to be having to teach its own inspectors.

Of course, it is possible to make a case that in a changing language we shouldn't talk about anything as forbidding as 'rules'. A. A. Gill, the brilliant television critic of the *Sunday Times*, says there were never any rules, only conventions and habits. Fair enough: I don't need to go to the stake in defence of 'rules' rather than 'conventions'. But people who press this point then leap to the claim that anything goes. Here's how Gill put it in the course of writing a typically robust attack on a BBC programme *Never Mind the Full Stops* presented by the writer Julian Fellowes.

> Nobody speaks better English than you do, whatever
> they say or however they say it. The language doesn't
> belong to Lynne Truss, Julian Fellowes, Fowler, the
> BBC or the Queen. It belongs to everyone who has
> something interesting to say.

Notice something about that little extract? Yes, Gill
has observed the rules (sorry, conventions). The punctuation is in the right place and the syntax would
satisfy the most pedantic critic. It is one of the many
reasons why his writing is so easy to read. Even if, as
he says, it has nothing to do with rules, only conven-
tion and habit, an interesting question arises. Gill, like
most good journalists, is an iconoclast, always challenging conventions and habits. So why does he not do
so when he's writing? Because he knows language is at
its best when there is no room for ambiguity and
misunderstanding, when it is clear and simple and
direct. Which is, of course, precisely why we have the
rules, the conventions and the habits. And long may
they be observed.

I am left with the impression that writers such as A.
A. Gill and experts such as David Crystal are rather
like people with a lot of money. They take it for
granted, cannot imagine what it must be like not to
have it so don't bother themselves with thinking about
those who have none. For 'money' read 'knowledge of
how to use language properly'. They have that knowledge and use it effortlessly, with style. But those who

don't have it struggle. And our common, shared world is the poorer because they do.

So my conclusion? Bring back grammar! And then we can all understand what is going on in our world.

CHAPTER TWO

The Legion of Little Lies

One of the nice things about knowing someone who's famous is being able to compare the public perception with the private man. John Simpson has won every award worth winning and I've no doubt the public perception of him is that he's brave, authoritative, intelligent and everything else that's needed to become the finest foreign correspondent of his generation. And all of that is true. But I've known John for thirty years – he's one of my closest friends – and there's something about him that most people probably don't know. We worked together in South Africa during the ghastly apartheid era and in Rhodesia during the final years of the guerrilla war, and one of the things that helped keep me sane was his sense of humour. Unlikely as it might seem when you watch him analysing the latest foreign crisis on television, John would have made a good stand-up comedian. He'd be brilliant as one of those characters who assumes the guise of someone he despises and exaggerates it to the point of ridicule.

There are risks in this. We once had dinner in a Rhodesian restaurant with a reporter who'd come out from London a few days earlier. John began playing the part of a typical Rhodesian 'redneck' – one of those characters who had settled in the country because he rather liked the idea of having lots of black servants to boss around and expected the 'blicks' to treat him with respect for no better reason than the colour of his skin. It had become a form of escape mechanism for both of us. But the reporter didn't get the joke. Maybe we should have warned him. Anyway, after ten minutes or so he leaped to his feet and rushed out of the restaurant. When we got back to the hotel where we were all staying we found he'd checked out and was on his way to the airport, complaining bitterly to anyone who'd listen about how Simpson and Humphrys had 'gone native' and become more racist than the 'rednecks'. We were a bit more careful after that.

John also writes wonderfully funny letters. I remember one he sent me shortly after he'd returned to London to become political editor of the BBC. He loathed the job and tore into the politicians and his new colleagues with savage humour. So when I had another letter from him recently I was puzzled. It was written on the headed paper of Roehampton University. It began:

> I am very excited to have been appointed Chancellor of Roehampton University and hope you will be able to join me at a ceremony to celebrate my new role.

There was something odd about this. Not that the university should have chosen John for the job or that he should have taken it. Anyone who saw him in his burka in Afghanistan will know that he'd enjoy the dressing-up bit, and obviously he would bring great gravitas and authority to the role. No, it was the language. He would have been flattered to be asked – even honoured – but 'very excited'? This is the man who liberated Kabul, who's been shot at and blown up more times than a firing-range target, and was once attacked by 'friendly' American fighters in Iraq; he bears the scars to this day. This is the man who can't see a war without wanting to be a part of it. He's so used to living dangerously he even had another baby when he was in his sixties. So was he 'very excited' to be appointed to a ceremonial post that required him to hand out degrees once a year and chair the occasional meeting? I don't think so. This was how the letter ended:

I do hope you will be able to join us for what I'm sure will be a fun event.

A 'fun event'! Did that mean there would be a tombola during the Latin oration and an egg-and-spoon race while all the mortar-boards were being doffed? Perhaps the vice chancellor was going to do a pole dance instead of the usual speech and the new graduates a spot of mud-wrestling. I doubt it. The more mundane explanation was that John had not written the letter at all. He had given the university a list of names while he was rushing off to another war and the letters were sent out on his behalf – which explains the hype.

I had another invitation that week – this time to a debate about libel law between lawyers and journalists. It said:

> Join us for a heated discussion when we will ask how
> far we can really go!

How did they *know* it was going to be 'heated', and did they assume no one would turn up if they'd merely promised it would be enlightening or helpful? Hype again.

Of course there has always been hype. It has been with us since the birth of the modern advertising and marketing industry: a low-level noise to which we have become so accustomed we pay it barely any attention. What is different now is that it has moved beyond the world of the hucksters who are obviously trying to sell us something and has become pervasive. Hence the use of hype in the academic world. It has also become so much more . . . well . . . hyper. Maybe that's inevitable. The more of it there is, the more we become inured to it and the higher they have to raise the bar. The supermarkets are the masters of the art – always trying to persuade us how thrilling it will be if we share our shopping experience with them. Note 'experience'. We don't go shopping any longer. We have an 'experience'. This is typical of supermarket hype:

Exciting changes to your Nectar card!

That's the promise from Sainsbury's contained in one of those irritating flyers that fall out of news-papers and utility bills. What can they possibly be offering that's so exciting? A chance to do your next big shop for free, maybe, or a case of vintage cham-pagne with every purchase over a fiver? Or even a guarantee that you won't have to wait for more than an hour at the check-out unless you do your shopping at three a.m. on Sunday? Not exactly. All is revealed in the next paragraph:

Ever wished you could use your Nectar points in more than just one Sainsbury's store?

As it happens, I've wished for many things in my life. I could probably offer you a list of a hundred things right now – everything from world peace and an end to poverty to a really good pint of bitter. But if I ever gave it a thought – which I haven't – I suppose I assumed that a giant supermarket chain with compu-ters powerful enough to map the human genome had probably already made it possible for me to use my points in more than one of their stores. That's assum-ing I had any points in the first place – which I haven't because my local market and corner shops supply everything I need and (whisper it quietly) often more cheaply. This sort of thing gives hype a bad name.

I know a man who works in the furniture business

(strictly upmarket stuff) and once allowed a Sunday colour supplement to do a feature on his loft apartment. Incidentally, it seems that 'apartment' has finally taken over from 'flat'; I fancy they'll soon have 'closets' rather than wardrobes. Anyway, he'd done a big conversion job on the loft and he thought the story might drum up some business for him. How naïve. When he opened the magazine he discovered that his rather elegant home had become a 'House of Fun'. Worse, the strapline read that he had

turned a morgue into a space that knows how to party.

This puzzled him a bit – partly because he couldn't quite picture a partying flat, but also because he hadn't had a party there for four years. And that had been a pretty sedate affair. Hype again. Or maybe it was just a bit of creative imagination. Isn't that what writers must do if they are to have any impact?

Well, it depends on the writer. Here's a job advertisement that appeared in the spring of 2006. The bold heading read:

Create the Words to Communicate Britain's Health Policy

The job was as Patricia Hewitt's speechwriter. It may seem a touch pedantic to complain that a speechwriter does not 'create' words but uses existing ones to create a speech, but the phrase 'create the words' needs looking at. It implies that the words will not have the usual relationship to what they're supposed to describe. In other words, what is really needed is the ability to hype. It goes on:

> In this pivotal role, you will draft speeches for the Secretary of State . . .

'Pivotal' is a wonderful word and itself is full of hype. It suggests the world revolves around you, that nothing can happen unless you are at the centre of things. That the word 'pivotal' brings to mind spin is surely coincidental. And there was more:

> Demonstrable ability to craft lucid, coherent and persuasive speeches for senior politicians is crucial, tailored to the needs of differing audiences at high profile conferences, set pieces, lectures, seminars, debates and other significant occasions.

Let's pass over the bad English (is it the 'ability' or the 'speeches' that must be tailored?) and consider how many buzz-words employed in the services of hype are in that short paragraph. 'Crucial'. 'High profile'. 'Significant occasions'. But the phrase I particularly liked was:

> tailored to the needs

'Tailored' is a fine, relatively recent hype word conveying a sense of the meticulous, the personal, the pin in the mouth to make sure it all fits quite perfectly. No ordinary, straightforward, off-the-peg speeches for the Secretary of State. And what's this about the 'needs of differing audiences'? I wonder if anyone ever 'needs' a speech. Try to imagine them leaving the hall after an hour of Mrs Hewitt or any other politician and saying: 'By God, I needed that!' They may have appreciated it or even enjoyed it. They may have hated it. But did they 'need' it? I very much doubt it. The 'needs', of course, are those of the boss.

But for me the Big Daddy in the advertisement is the use of the word 'craft'. It transports us to the world of sawdust-strewn workshops and gnarled old artisans chiselling and sawing away, creating beautiful pieces of furniture using skills handed down over the generations. The work of a real craftsman speaks for itself – no hype needed.

Oddly enough, that's not quite how I picture politicians' speechwriters at work. Not that I'd go as far as George Orwell, who once wrote that political language 'is designed to make lies sound truthful and murder respectable and to give an appearance of solidity to pure wind'. It's hard not to imagine that the word 'crafty' was floating around in the mind of the person who put 'craft' in the advertising copy.

There is at least one word in the advertisement that means what it says and says what it means: 'persuasive'. Indeed, persuasion is the only 'skill' that's truly essential. If the politician is able to persuade the audience, the mission has been accomplished.

I suppose the job vacancy was filled pretty quickly. Certainly it paid well: £56,543 for an eighteen-hour week. Speech-writing doesn't come cheap, which is fair enough if it plays an important part in conveying politicians' arguments and giving us a better understanding of what they are trying to do on our behalf. But audiences, in my experience, have an unerring ability to sniff out hype and spot when a speech they are listening to has been written by someone other than the person who's delivering it. And they don't like it. They want to feel that the politician has been speaking from the heart, rather than faithfully regurgitating the words of a civil servant or highly paid adviser. Sounds obvious, but it's remarkable how many politicians go through the motions of delivering a speech even though they know they're probably more likely to be alienating their audience than persuading them.

The language of hype does not come with a big flashing sign saying, 'Hi, sucker!' Its vocabulary is limited to remarkably few familiar words: 'brilliant'; 'exciting'; 'fun'; 'simple'. But the users of hype need to be careful. Some of their words can be seriously dangerous. Take, for example, a favourite of theirs: 'perfect'. We stopped being perfect around the time when Eve picked the apple and started coming on to Adam. That has not stopped some NHS hospitals signing up to a scheme called 'Pursuing Perfection'.

One found itself in the headlines because it could not afford to pay enough porters and the bodies of patients who had died during the night were being left in their beds because there was no one to take them to the mortuary.

Among the most cherished words in the lexicon of hype is 'great'. If you took 'great' away from your average hypester, it would be like snatching a life-belt from a drowning man. Try flicking through one of those wretched advertising inserts next time and count how often it's used. But sometimes this tediously overused adjective finds itself attached to some very strange words. Try this, for example:

> We'd like to say to people: 'We're warm and breath-ing. We've got great product. Come and have a look.'

Those are the words of Stuart Rose, one of the best retailers in the business. He's the man who took over Marks & Spencer when it was on its knees and put it back on its feet. But 'great product'? Great knickers maybe, or great skirts, or even great fishcakes, but has anyone in the real world ever, ever said to anyone else, 'I really must nip into M&S. I'm told they've got great product'? And it's not as if Mr Rose is one of those executives who seems to be incapable of speaking a language we all understand. Here's how he described a disastrous revamp of the big M&S store in Birming-ham:

'We screwed up big time. We pissed off a lot of customers.'

Not, perhaps, the language he might use in polite company, but it doesn't half tell it like it is. And I'd imagine that anyone who'd had an unhappy experience in the Birmingham store would greatly appreciate a bit of plain speaking. But plain speaking is to hype what garlic is to Dracula. I enjoyed (in a masochistic sort of way) the questionnaire on a Virgin train that came with the menu. It assured me, as these things invariably do, that Virgin were 'constantly seeking' to improve the service. The reason it wanted my 'feedback' was . . .

. . . so that we can ensure that we are meeting your needs, and exceeding your expectations.

Do people who write this stuff ever read their own words? If they are constantly seeking to exceed my expectations we're going to find ourselves in a gastronomic race in which they'll soon be having to serve me larks' tongues in aspic to stop me suing them for false trading. But even in the midst of such mindless hype, language can bring us down to reality with a thud. The menu itself was

. . . recommended for customers on shorter journeys, and for those who do not want to be interrupted as all components will be delivered at the same time.

Whatever happened to 'courses'? I've never thought of eating 'components'. We're back in the world of 'product'. But let's be charitable – if not sympathetic. After all, the menu was signed by the managing director, one Charles Belcher. You think he eats his own 'components' too quickly?

It's nice, though, isn't it, knowing that all these hotshot executives feel so close to their customers? A letter I received from BT was signed 'Kind regards'. True, it wasn't actually addressed to me (or anyone else for that matter) but it's the thought that counts. And it's good that they are so 'committed'. That's another favourite hype word. This letter began:

> At BT, we are committed to providing great value for all our customers, by constantly developing in-novative new products and delivering high quality services.

'Great value', eh? Sounds good. A few quid off the next bill never comes amiss. But here's how my new friend at BT went on:

> To continue to do this, it's occasionally necessary to raise some of our prices a little.

Ah, I see. 'Great value', in this Lewis Carroll world, means higher prices. But what about these 'innovative new products'? I assumed that in the fast-moving world of telecoms that meant at least, say, better phones with batteries that lasted longer or little head-

sets you could wear when you were wandering around
the house chatting on your cordless phone. This is
what they mean:

> Customers on BT Together Option 2 or 3 can now
> benefit from savings. By signing up to a 12 month
> contract, you save £33 (£5.50 a month – that's half
> the price of BT Together Option 1 line rental £11**).
> So you pay only £11** for Option 2 (usually
> £16.50**), or £20** for Option 3 (usually
> £25.50**), for the first six months.

I'll spare you the detail of the asterisks just as I spared
myself. It is entirely possible that, buried somewhere
in that impenetrable paragraph, is a deal that really
would 'meet my needs'. But I shall never find out
because life is simply too short to spend precious hours
trying to work it out. Sooner or later one loses the will
to live. I feel the same about all those terribly tempting
offers to buy my electricity and gas from somebody
else. I managed to pass maths at O level half a century
ago, but only just.

You need much more than an ancient maths O level
to deal with train fares. I've just been listening to a
man from the Association of Train Operating Companies trying to justify the ludicrous complexity of
them. Twenty years ago there were five types of ticket
on sale. Now the National Fares Manual lists more
than seventy fares governed by 776 'validity' condi-
tions. The result is that no one (with the possible

exception of the people who run the railways) can make head or tail of them. Certainly not the passengers – or 'customers', as we must now be described. Yet the man from the ATOC insisted over and over again that the fares really do 'suit the needs' (that word again) of the passengers because so many people travel by train. Well, of *course* they do! They *need* to get to work.

It is vaguely reassuring to know that I am not alone in finding all this choice so off-putting, so alien to my real needs. Whole companies exist to help us, the wretched 'consumers', decide which supplier provides the best value for money. Wouldn't it be wonderful if the rail companies, the telecom operators and the energy suppliers threw all their 'innovative new products' in the bin and came up with something simple. Imagine if they were to say to us: 'Here's what it will cost you for every mile you travel / every unit of electricity you use / every minute you're on the phone.' Obviously we would pay more in peak times; we have always done so and we know why it's necessary. But if it were to be simplified, we'd be able to understand what we were being offered and we could make informed choices. Of course, that will never happen and the reason lies in one word. Hype.

Hype is everywhere. It has even infiltrated what I still think of as the musty offices of HM Customs & Revenue (the Inland Revenue in old money). They decided recently they needed a new marketing manager to 'build the campaigns that build our image'. You may wonder why. However you wrap it up, what the taxman does is take money from us. Nothing wrong with that. We may not enjoy paying tax but we know it's necessary. It may occur to you that the money they spend on marketing is our money and the more they spend, the more they have to take from us, but here's the bit of hype I liked: HM Revenue is

> . . . working with the largest customer base of any UK organisation.

Well, yes, they would be, wouldn't they? For the very simple reason that we have no choice. If we choose not to be their 'customer' there's absolutely nothing we can do about it. So why make such a daft boast? You know the answer.

There was a time when hype was the job of the company's marketing department. Sadly, it is now required of everyone: the bank manager; the hospital chief executive; the head teacher; the airline pilot. Yes, the airline pilot. Here we are, locked into a metal tube hurtling through the air at 550 mph at 33,000 feet, aware that it's so cold outside we'll be dead in ten seconds if a window falls out, worrying whether that shifty bloke in the row in front has a bomb in his shoe, and we're invited to 'sit back, relax and enjoy ourselves' because

'Looking after you today we have a GREAT team!'

That presumably means that the team yesterday was rubbish. There does seem to have been a slight variation in airline language recently. Instead of 'enjoying the flight' we are often enjoined to enjoy 'the service'. Now, this is seriously perverse. It may be possible to enjoy the service if you had turned left when you boarded the plane and your only problem is which claret to select with your meal before turning your seat into a comfortable bed, but not if you are in cattle class becoming increasingly annoyed by all those stupid announcements telling you to enjoy yourself.

Especially annoying is the one that says they're about to try to flog you duty-free goods, which you will already have bought at the airport or will buy in the local market when you arrive at your foreign destination. Not that they put it like that. Instead they tell you that 'passing down the aisle' is what I have heard called an 'in-flight retail facilitator'.

Goebbels said that if you repeat a big lie often enough it becomes the truth. The sort of stuff I've been sounding off about is not made up of big lies. Hype doesn't work like that. It's about a legion of little ones. The insidious thing about hype is not so much that it pretends that something is what it's not.

58

It's rather that the sheer pervasiveness of the language of hype does indeed 're-create' what is around us so that we get used to seeing it in its terms. Hype may often seem just funny, even preposterous. But it colours a large part of the world we're living in and, for all its crudeness, subtly changes its nature.

CHAPTER THREE

Are You Shopping Comfortably?

In theory, one of the nice things about being on the radio and television is that you get lots of invitations to parties. I say 'in theory' because I can't quite see the fun in standing around for two hours drinking mediocre wine and spending exactly four and a half minutes talking to a succession of people whose names you can't remember. After four and a half minutes – at the precise point when you think you're about to remember the name and the conversation begins to get interesting – someone else comes along (whose name you also can't remember), chips in and you have to talk to them. There is sometimes a variation on this theme. This involves talking to someone who is so famous you really *do* know him, but who obviously finds you insufficiently famous to justify wasting his time and spends the four and a half minutes looking over your shoulder, hoping to find someone more important.

It is one of the mysteries of modern life that so many organisations waste so much time and money staging these grisly events, even though nobody ever admits to enjoying them but thinks they should 'put in an appearance'. Which takes me to the other nice thing about presenting a breakfast programme. It means you can turn down the invitations on the basis that you have to get up too early. So you get invited, which is nice because it makes you feel important and loved, but you don't have to go and can stay at home with a good book, which is even nicer – and you don't offend anyone. Perfect, really.

I had an invitation the other day to something that looked as if it might be reasonably interesting. It was an 'AWARENESS EVENT!'. These things always have capital letters and exclamation marks. How else would we know they were exciting? But I'd never been to an 'awareness event' before so I read on. It sounded pretty good. There was even a reward for going: two free plane tickets to a pleasant part of Spain with overnight accommodation thrown in. Yes, you've guessed, they were trying to flog me a time-share development. Obviously there's nothing new in hyping these things. Time-share hucksters get such a bad press – usually for very good reasons – that they need to keep coming up with something new to get us hooked. But why did they call it an 'awareness event'? If it had to be an 'event' at all, why couldn't it be an 'information event'?

Answer: because their marketing department would have told anyone who came up with such a boring, straightforward suggestion that they really had to start thinking outside the box, have a little imagination, jazz it up a bit. Information is dreary. It sounds so formal and serious. Also, give people information and they get picky: they start asking awkward questions. You don't want that. You want to flatter the punters a bit: any old fool can handle information – but 'awareness'? That's for a special kind of person. And awareness is not something you pick apart, it's something you just, like, accept and respect. Know what I'm saying?

I'm sorry to lurch into *faux*-American but I find it difficult to come across the word 'awareness' used in this way without imagining a bunch of Californians sitting around for hours talking in a monotone, never saying a word that might be even faintly politically incorrect, nodding in sympathetic understanding at everything and never once collapsing into giggles at the absurdity of it all.

Used in this way, the word changes direction by 180 degrees. Instead of referring to an awareness *of* something, it turns right round, ignores what's out there and concentrates on the person doing the aware-ing, so to speak. Awareness is all about an inner state.

It's rather like the word 'enjoy'. You're sitting in a restaurant, the waitress brings your meal and, with a sweet smile, says, 'Enjoy!' I want to say: 'Don't you know that "enjoy" is a transitive not an intransitive verb? You should say, "Enjoy it!" not "Enjoy!". Whatever do they teach in Polish schools, these days?'

As with 'awareness', the new, fashionable 'enjoy' makes our own experience, rather than the meal, the centre of attention. The message is clear. In a world of 'enjoy' and 'awareness' (rather than information), inner personal experience is what we must be thinking about – rather than what's out there.

But that's only right. Remember, all we're here for is to shop.

> 'Now, when I go out and buy a pair of trainers, they are not only cool, but some of the profits are going to raise awareness.'

That curious sentence came from the luscious lips of the actress Scarlett Johansson. She was talking about RED – capital letters again, I'm afraid, but that's how it's spelled. Bono, the singer who is famous enough to wear sunglasses indoors without everyone laughing at him, is the inspiration behind RED. You may remember him talking about it at the Live 8 concert in the summer of 2005. He got a group of companies together to sell some of their products under the RED label. Ms Johansson didn't get it quite right. The profits are not spent on raising awareness but will go into the Global Fund, which fights TB, Aids and malaria in Africa. And a very good thing too. But without wishing to be curmudgeonly about this, 'awareness' (in the old-fashioned sense of the word) doesn't appear to have an awful lot to do with it. Ms Johansson again:

'It's an available way of helping others, especially when you're doing something that's kind of mindless, like shopping. You don't have to write a cheque or travel to Africa to contribute, you can help out in your daily routine.'

It's true we can't all go to Africa to see what's happening for ourselves, but somehow the 'daily routine' of flashing our American Express RED card doesn't strike me as being very likely to increase our awareness of what's going on in the dark continent. And if it's *instead* of 'having to write a cheque' every now and then, it could be said to have the opposite effect. Here's how American Express put it in full-page newspaper advertisements:

Can desire ever have a virtuous side?

Or, does popular theory prevail that it can only exist in spite of virtue? RED flies in the face of popular theory and believes Desire can be Virtuous. That's why we created the American Express RED card.

Let us resist the temptation to think ignoble thoughts here and put behind us any suggestion that American Express might see some commercial advantage in proclaiming its virtuous side. Anything that raises money for such a worthwhile cause must be a good thing. What's fascinating is the notion that desire – or 'spoiling yourself', as the advertisement puts it –

can be virtuous. Maybe Ms Johansson got it right. After all, an 'awareness' is being created – the awareness that we are truly virtuous people and can demonstrate it to ourselves without actually having to make the slightest sacrifice. Virtue does indeed have its own reward if we can prove we are charitable without making any effort and without it costing us a bean. This is how the article about RED in a Sunday supplement put it:

. . . the shopping revolution that's good for the soul.

It turns out that this shopping revolution (or 'conscience consumerism', as it's also called) is not so much about awareness of the world out there as about the soul in you. And, it hardly needs adding, what's meant by 'good for the soul', these days, is no more and no less than feeling good about yourself. Feelgood is salvation and the daily routine of tending to the soul is not saying a few Hail Marys or writing out a cheque for charity but, well, shopping. You could call it the New Awareness. Enjoy!

To return to the point about capital letters, it's a couple of centuries since nouns in the English language were routinely capitalised – not that anyone seems to have told American Express. But mostly we do the opposite now. It seems obligatory for 'rebranded' companies to have their name in lower case. Publicity material often gives lower-case letters to words in sentences that scream out for a capital. This is the title of an introductory brochure to LA Fitness gyms in London:

welcome! To your LA Journey

This is positively perverse. If ever a word demanded a capital it's that 'welcome!'. It cannot be an accident – the writer's finger slipping off the shift key – because someone would have noticed, wouldn't they? Perhaps one day a learned academic will construct an elegant theory around this sort of thing. My own view is that life's too short. I shall punish them by not joining an LA Fitness gym – which is not a massive sacrifice, given that I have never been much attracted to the smell of stale sweat, the sound of endless TV monitors blasting out hideous music and the sight of muscle-bound men showing off with those funny wide belts around their rippling stomachs. A trot around my local park suits me very nicely, thank you.

'Journey', you will have noticed, does have a capital letter. It's another of those gooey words like 'awareness'. It has an obvious physical meaning and, if you happen to be into this sort of thing, a metaphysical one too: life as a journey, the soul struggling along a path to . . . who knows where? There's another thesis to be written on that, but possibly not the sort of thing the gym people had in mind. For most people the gym 'journey' is a brief one. At approximately midday on 1

January they read the lifestyle articles in the news-papers, contemplate the amount of food and booze they have managed to consume over the past ten days and the effect it has had on their flabby bodies, and sign up at a gym. Some of them might even go more than once. But not many. It usually turns out to be a very short journey indeed.

But even more interesting than 'Journey' in the brochure title is the word 'your'. This little fellow is elbowing his way into everything, an insistent reminder of how things have changed. Where the world once consisted of lots of different things, free-standing and independent and among which 'you' were just one in six billion, now everything is presented as though it were just an extension of you, existing only as part of 'your personal experience'. Ms Johansson teaches us that. Marks & Spencer may have 'great product' but it also has a newish slogan:

Your M&S

It is disarmingly simple and it is untrue. M&S does not belong to the customers: it belongs to the share-holders. As the writer Lucy Kellaway points out, it 'implies that the product or service has been specially designed just for you personally'. It hasn't. The stuff is mass-produced for a mass market and the business – like almost every other large business around the world – is becoming less and less personal. Products are 'increasingly global and customer service is conducted via voicemail – or by a worker in India reading from a prompt sheet'. The splendid Ms Kellaway, incidentally, writes for the *Financial Times* – or rather, as it has taken to describing itself, 'Your *FT*'.

Words such as 'you' and 'yours' create a virtual reality that is very convenient for those who use them. They blur the edges of that awkward little space between two distinct players: the company and the customer. It is in this space that difficult questions get asked and conflict might break out. That danger is reduced if we are told: 'Look, it's not ours or someone else's. It's YOURS.' As the 'new awareness' tells us, 'you' are the central reference point of modern life, so why should you question what 'we' do on your behalf?

What all this concentration on 'you' is doing is reversing the Copernican revolution. You'll remember that Copernicus pointed out that the Earth wasn't the centre of the universe; it was just a planet orbiting the sun. And we now know there are billions of such suns, which makes us humans, perched on one little planet, pretty insignificant in the scheme of things. But that's not how we are encouraged to see matters any more. The new geography of the universe has You at the centre of it and around You is a comfort zone in which You should feel good about Yourself.

Advertising peddles this line all the time.

There's an advertisement for Italian furniture with a picture of a beautiful young couple relaxing in their elegant living room. The woman is stretched out on the sofa, the man squatting beside her, pouring tea into cups on a low table. The words over the picture read:

Comfort. Around You. Within You.

That's as good a definition as you will get of the comfort zone: we are encouraged to believe that the world should be exclusively for us. An inner sense of feeling comfortable about ourselves stretches out into the physical space we occupy. It may make you want to pour the hot tea down the front of the man's trousers and snap: 'Still feeling comfort within you?' But that would just show you are not keeping up with the times – which is similar to the feeling I have when politicians or their little helpers use such crass language.

The word 'comfortable' has had its own interesting career recently. At some point in the last couple of years – it's always hard to be specific in these cases – politicians and public servants started to be 'comfortable' with things. Usually it's a spin doctor or PR type who will tell you that the boss is 'comfortable' with this or that decision. It's a troubling phrase. It implies that the politician's peace of mind is what really matters – rather than whether the decision was right or wrong. It probably came from the United States and invites that curious Californian response again: the head nodding very slowly and a long-drawn-out 'riiiight'. It also invites a smart slap. Keeping democracy going is quite difficult in a 'comfort zone'.

But, not for the first time, we must turn to the world of showbiz and celebrities to take us a step further. The singer Cher decided to sell off some old junk – actually some pretty valuable stuff, including decent paintings and ballgowns that she'd had for years. You or I might have called it a 'clearout'. She called it

'rewriting my personal environment'

I imagine it remains quite comfortable.

Some of you, though, may require some guidance about how to make your life's comfort zone yet more comfortable. In that case what you need is 'Life Coaching'. I saw an advertisement for 'complimentary' life coaching, no less, which read:

An Executive Life coach can truly be, do or have anything you want. Unlock your potential!

Of course it was the execrable grammar that caught my attention but can it really be the case that just by hiring a coach I can 'be, do or have' anything I want?

If you are still not persuaded that, in our contemporary world, you really do sit at the centre of the universe in your very own comfort zone, able to command whatever you want, let me refer you to a higher authority, Noel Edmonds. His broadcasting career went through a lean patch when the gates of

Crinkly Bottom were finally slammed shut, but he was rescued by the startling success of *Deal or No Deal*. Let him who would cast the first stone at such a pointless use of television air time be prepared to admit that he has never been hooked by it!

Mr Edmonds is a formidable broadcaster but it seems he owes his success to more than his ability and a piece of inspired television scheduling. Cosmic ordering must be taken into the equation too – or, at least, he thinks so. It is all about asking the universe (the 'cosmos') for the things you want in life. This bizarre notion has been popularised by the writer Barbel Mohr, and her book, *The Cosmic Ordering Service*, has sold approximately a zillion copies. A modest lady, Ms Mohr, she even says that just by holding her book in your hand you have already 'changed your life'. Here's the pitch:

> Are you still waiting for your ship to come in? Looking for the relationship you can't seem to find? Working just to pay the bills until that perfect job comes along? Don't you wish that you could just place an order for the life you want? Well, Barbel Mohr says you can! And you don't have to chant, meditate, pray, fast, work, or do anything – just relax. And there won't be any bill to pay.

One of her many disciples in this country, Georgina Davies, told the *Daily Mail* that it works for her:

How you place an order is up to you, but rather than say 'I want more money', I imagined myself being rich. The next day my mother phoned and announced she wanted to pay for me to have a weekend away, I got a tax rebate of £700 and I also got two modelling jobs – all on the same day.

And no request is too trivial. Here's another believer, Heather Price:

From finding a parking space in a busy car park to landing the job of my dreams, cosmic ordering has brought many positive things into my life.

Including, it seems, her boyfriend:

Until then, I'd always gone for men I'd end up having unhealthy, possessive relationships with. I asked the cosmos to bring me a relationship in which we could both allow each other to be free and not make unrealistic demands on each other. I met my current boyfriend the week after making the order and we've been together for three years.

Georgina Davies ordered up her boyfriend too, but there must have been some crossed wires somewhere:

The only thing I asked for that didn't match was that he be called Jake – my favourite man's name. In fact he's called Pete, but I don't really think that's something to complain about. Cosmic ordering means I never have to worry about anything, because it's given me an ability to trust that everything will work out exactly how I would like it to.

Hmm. I'm not sure Ms Davies was wise to accept a Pete when she wanted a Jake. He may well be a decent bloke, but it's the principle of the thing. Give 'em an inch and they'll take a mile. Next thing you know that cosmos crowd will want to be paid for the goods – even if they're defective.

I know it's easy to poke fun at all this (not that that's any reason we shouldn't) and I know there will always be people prepared to believe the moon is made of green cheese if a 'best-selling' book tells them so, but there's a serious point to be made. It's the notion that consumerism has finally taken over our way of understanding everything. The universe turns out to be a giant warehouse sitting somewhere out there, ready to supply all our needs without us having to make the slightest effort on our own behalf – not even a little prayer now and then. The cosmos as a just-in-time delivery service waiting to hear what we want perfectly fits the fiction of a comfort zone with ourselves and our appetites at its centre. It's all of a piece with the language of 'awareness' and 'journeys' and 'your' this and 'your' that and 'shopping revolutions' that are good for the soul.

But just in case I'm wrong, I've written out my own cosmic order and put it under my pillow. Well, you'd feel a fool if you didn't and it really worked, wouldn't you? So if you didn't hear me on the radio this morning it's probably because I'm a bit busy writing the acceptance speech for my Nobel Prize . . .

CHAPTER FOUR

Get a Lifestyle!

It's almost thirty years since I started presenting the *Nine O'Clock News* on BBC1. That was in the days when news studios did not resemble the inside of the Tardis just before take-off and newsreaders were not required to strut around the place looking like superannuated shop-walkers. My bosses assumed that the viewers were perfectly capable of following the news if it was read by someone sitting behind a desk instead of standing in front of vast screens, waving their arms a great deal and pointing at things. Nor did they much care what we wore. It's true that I was told to buy a new suit (even though the one I'd bought for my wedding fifteen years earlier was still perfectly good) but I never actually wore a suit on air – just the jacket. Since newsreaders were never seen below the waist, I tended to wear old jeans.

A few years ago a call came from Light Entertainment – known to everyone in the business as LE – asking me to present *Mastermind*. This is the glamorous bit of the BBC. If News is a fairly ropy (but reliable) old Ford, LE is a flashy Lamborghini. At LE they *do* care what you wear. And how. So I wasn't unduly surprised when, a few weeks before the first programme, I had a call from a young man in LE asking me if I'd spend the day with him shopping for new clothes. I needed, it seems, a 'makeover'. I would like to say that I resisted and that I pulled the same 'I've got a perfectly good suit' line from thirty years ago. But I didn't. When someone treats you like a star – which they most emphatically do not in News – it's difficult to resist. And, after a few muted protests, I loved it. I discovered what every woman knows from birth: clothes *do* make you feel different. If you march out on to the studio floor knowing that you're now in the entertainment business – even if *Mastermind* is at the serious end of it – it gives you a little boost to know that your clothes don't look as though they've come from a charity shop and your jacket could do with a visit to the dry cleaner's. I have even – possibly for the first time in my life – been complimented on my dress sense by one or two people below the age of thirty.

This is the relatively innocent aspect of the make-over culture. I use the word 'culture' because makeovers have taken over. Until relatively recently the word 'makeover' did not even appear in the dictionary – much less in the television schedules. Imagine the vast stretches of blank screen over the past few years if makeover shows had been removed. Everything gets one now. And the sinister truth behind them is that it's not just our houses or our wardrobes or our gardens that they are designed to change. It's us. It is *we* who need makeovers, who must be fashioned anew. Or, to use another word that has entered the dictionary only recently, it is our 'lifestyles' that need the makeover. And, as every student of modern culture knows, lifestyles are far more important than lives.

The shift is reflected in language. Sometimes you stumble across sentences that simply could not have been written twenty years ago. Here's one, from an upmarket newspaper:

> We like to connect with the values of the snowboarding lifestyle.

This bizarre sentence needs a bit of unpacking. Even those addicted to snowboarding may scratch their heads about why standing on a board and hurtling down a snow slope should constitute a lifestyle, as distinct from something you might just do every now and again. Even odder, why should such an activity, whether it constitutes a lifestyle or not, have 'values'? And what exactly are they? Honour? Loyalty? Frugality? Concern for others?

But perhaps the oddest bit of the sentence is the use of 'connect with' in relation to values. As I've always understood values, you might want to adopt them, or deplore them, or live by them, or preach them, but what has this timidly noncommittal phrase 'connect with' to do with values?

It might help to know who spoke the words: Anne Nenonen, the senior manager of global marketing at

Nokia, the mobile-phone company. She was explaining to the *Financial Times* how brands like hers seek out quirky action sports such as snowboarding and try to gain kudos with the punters by providing the sport with corporate sponsorship. Why the 'snowboarding lifestyle' should be important was explained by Casey Wasserman, the chairman and chief executive of Wasserman Media Group, who said of the snowboarders:

> 'This coveted and valuable audience with disposable income, a propensity to drink colas, energy drinks and bottled water, communicate using mobile devices, or wear fashionable shoes, shirts and shorts has become elusive.'

It makes them sound like a clandestine sect or, perhaps, a troop of rare baboons. You can picture David Attenborough spying on them from the undergrowth and whispering to the camera: 'This elusive animal with its extraordinary behaviour – so rarely seen outside its usual habitat of Notting Hill wine bars – gives us a fascinating glimpse into a world of which we know so little.' Once people are defined by their lifestyle they become what is known in the trade as a 'demographic'.

The snowboarding demographic, naturally enough, has its own values – or so the Wassermans of this world would have us believe. Except, of course, that in the real world values attach to life. When it's lifestyle we're talking about it's a different kettle of fish. As Joe Queenan, author of *Balsamic Dreams*, has put it:

> 'The measure of human success is no longer the life well lived but the lifestyle well lived.'

Lifestyle is a bit like football in the sense that it brings to mind that hoary old gag of Bill Shankly, the legendary manager of Liverpool, when he was asked about the game being a matter of life and death. 'No,' he said, 'it's more important than that.' Or maybe it's better represented by the young man in the jeweller's shop trying to buy his girlfriend the current must-have fashion accessory – a chain with a silver cross. He'd looked through dozens without finding what he wanted and the assistant asked what the problem was. 'Yeah, these are all right,' he said, 'but I really want one of them crosses with the little feller on.'

But there is no dodging the questions posed by Queenan's remark. What *is* the 'lifestyle well lived'? Ah, well, that depends on whether you're a 'civilian' – which is how Liz Hurley allegedly referred to those unfortunates who, unlike her, are not clothed in the mantle of celebrity. We should, perhaps, pass quickly over the fact that her celebrity is not exactly unrelated to her frequent appearances in public clothed in very little – most famously just a few scraps of cloth and some large safety-pins. Either way, the use of the insidiously patronising word 'civilians' in this context has caught on among the celebrity set. Anyway, the social classification is a little more complex.

Between celebrities and civilians sits another group. 'Sublebrities' is the word coined by the excellent Marina Hyde of *The Guardian*. It means civilians who have had a shot at becoming celebrities but not quite made it. Not that there is any shortage of 'real' celebrities. I had dinner with Marina a few days after she'd been asked by her paper to write a weekly column about the strange world celebrities inhabit. She was terrified that there would not be enough material to keep it going. She needn't have been. I suspect she'll be in a job long after Ms Hurley has fastened her last safety-pin.

So we now have a different social hierarchy from the one based on class and famously satirised by John Cleese, Ronnie Barker and Ronnie Corbett. Cleese was the upper-class character and he looked down on Barker, who looked up to him. Barker, who was middle class, looked down on Corbett, who looked up to both of them. A modern version would have Ms Hurley (a *real* celebrity) looking down on a wannabe celebrity – anyone who's been on *Big Brother* or *Pop Idol*, for instance. And in downtrodden little Ronnie Corbett's place, looking up to both of them, would be the equivalent of the check-out girl at the supermarket.

No doubt if you asked her whether she took celebrity life seriously, she'd say of course not, it's just a bit of a laugh. Except that you'll catch her poring over

Hello! magazine or doing herself up on a Friday night to look as much as possible like whoever happens to be adorning its pages. And perfectly serious newspapers are prepared to devote thousands of words to exploring the lives and opinions of people who have become celebrities for no better reason than that they married a footballer or pop star or enjoyed a fumble under the sheets at the *Big Brother* house. Celebrity life may be a fantasy but it's the dominant fantasy of our times.

In January 2006 the Learning and Skills Council reported that 16 per cent of the teenagers it had interviewed believed they would become famous, probably by appearing on shows like *Big Brother*. Many saw it as a better prospect than obtaining qualifications. They were sitting around 'waiting to be discovered'. The Council calculated that the chances of their actually becoming rich and famous as a result were roughly 30 million to one.

I don't suppose that made any difference because it is so hard to get away from it – as is clear from the phrase 'celebrity exposure'. Exposure was once something best avoided. You could die of it on a mountain or be destroyed by it in the red-top Sunday papers. These days it is usually grabbed with both hands. Enough exposure in the media (good or bad) can indeed guarantee an income for life – or at least until the papers tire of you, which will probably come sooner. Ask Rebecca Loos, who's done remarkably well out of sleeping (or not, as the case may be) with

David Beckham. Had it not been for all her exposure she might never have appeared on national television masturbating a pig. Let that be a lesson to us all.

There are moments in history when various elements come together to form the perfect combination. When the universe was young, hydrogen and oxygen fused to produce water. Life became possible. Messrs Rolls and Royce formed a partnership that gave us the finest cars and aircraft engines. Morecambe and Wise changed the face of television comedy. And then, in the summer of 2006, we witnessed the birth of a new force of nature. The WAGS were created.

Some people may affect outrage at the thought that the Wives and Girlfriends of the English footballers have earned themselves even a footnote in the history of this great nation. Well, let them. The WAGS had nothing more than their relationships (sometimes fleeting) with overpaid young footballers; extremely short skirts and long legs; the occasional surgical enhancement; a limitless capacity for booze and a truly heroic ability to shop. One more ingredient was needed in the mix.

As Laurel found his Hardy and Torville her Dean, so the WAGS found their partner: *the paparazzi*. A media starved of good British hooligan stories and with a desperate need to fill the many pages allocated by some Supreme Being to the non-event known as the World Cup provided the crucible in which this perfect partnership was fused. The English players themselves may have let down a nation, but not their partners. Marketing experts assured us that the girls would easily earn £5 million in the months after England's ignominious departure from Germany. Aleck Hornshaw of Get Me Media (I think we do) said: 'They have been catapulted into the limelight and will reap the benefits. They are aspirational figures and, from a marketing point of view, seriously hot property.' How right he was. One of the WAGS worked in a humble, low-paid job before Germany but after her exploits Mr Hornshaw assured us: 'She's a big star now.'

What turns stardom into hard cash is the opportunity to sponsor brands. As any half-awake follower of celebrities knows, an essential requirement of the celebrity lifestyle is always to use the right brands. The key here is to know precisely which celebrity is endorsing which brand at any given moment. Just a fleeting glimpse of a serious A-list celeb holding a particular handbag between limo and restaurant will do – even if she's only holding it for a friend. The PR people will do the rest.

Unlike 'makeover' and 'lifestyle', 'brand' is not a new word, but with its new friends it has acquired a whole new meaning. You could say it has had a makeover of its own. It comes from the Middle English word for 'burning'. In the sixteenth century it meant the mark made on something by burning it with a hot iron. The point about such a mark was that it was indelible. It provided a permanent means of identifying someone for what he was: a criminal, a slave. By the early nineteenth century and the beginnings of a consumer society, it had become a trade mark: again, the means of authenticating that something was what it was thought to be.

But 'brand' became bored with authenticity. Endlessly reassuring people that something is what it is thought to be and that no change has occurred – nor ever will – is hardly a life for an ambitious little word in such illustrious company. What if people could be persuaded to be less impressed by underlying realities and start instead to think what brand names might *suggest*? That would give some scope for the brand to conjure up all sorts of imaginary associations. Then we would start paying much more attention to these ephemeral but attractive associations than to dreary old reality.

Before long we would concentrate solely on appearances and forget all about realities. Eventually we might even come to believe that appearance *was* reality. Then brand would have ceased to be the dull slave of reality, authenticating that something was really what it seemed to be, and would have become the gadfly king of virtual reality, joking that anything could be anything, really.

Branding is now the art of getting people to think what something might be rather than what it necessarily is. It's about the manipulation of the virtual reality in which so many of us live. The manipulators include anyone with an interest in what we might think of them – not just big companies with products to sell but political parties with votes to win, design gurus with clients to attract – anyone, in other words, acting in some kind of market. They all have an interest in controlling their appearance to make us believe it is the reality.

Names are important if you want to control the image of your brand. The giant oil company, BP, has become 'bp', ridding itself of the imposing, powerful connotation of the capital letters in favour of the more modest, self-effacing manner of the lower-case. But it's gone further. In an audacious piece of rebranding, the company is trying to get us to think that the initials of its name do not stand, as we thought, for 'British Petroleum' but rather for 'beyond petroleum'.

It's not that this is a downright lie. BP is in the oil business and oil is running out. So it is spending serious money on exploring alternative sources of energy it hopes to sell us in the era 'beyond petroleum'. But the implication is that BP's vast profits have nothing to do with all that mucky oil that's polluting the Earth and everything to do with the pretty green and yellow flowers that adorn its winsome ads and are all part of branding it as a green company. Some makeover.

You might think that with such jiggery-pokery going on, branding needs to be a surreptitious activity in which the punters can't see the strings being pulled. Not a bit of it. In our post-modern world, where appearance is accepted as reality, the branding people seem to believe there's no harm in laying bare how their strange profession works. For many years a big chunk of the BBC was known as BBC Broadcast. It has changed its name – and is happy to tell us why:

> We wanted a name that reflected where we have come from. When we were Broadcasting and Presentation we were known as B&P. As BBC Broadcast we have been known as BBCB. So an evolutionary step was to play with the sound 'B'.
>
> The spelling as 'Bee' came from an internal brainstorm when we were looking at nature's expert navigators, because as a company facing the digital future we need to help the consumer become equally adept as navigators. We have always used Red as our colour property and this gave added strength to the name.
>
> We look forward to working with you as Red Bee Media.

Wonderful things, these brainstorms. But I'm leading us away from the important business of celebrity and how not to make a *faux pas* when selecting your own brands. That's important because your choice of brand is so vital in defining your identity. Neal Lawson, the chairman of the left-wing pressure group Compass, says we were once known by what we produced but now we judge ourselves and others by what we consume. It represents the triumph of the marketing men. The advertisers exploit it when they ask: 'What does your mobile say about you'?

It's such a pressing question you're going to need help.
No one is more capable of giving advice on keeping abreast of the celebrity lifestyle than Tyler Brûlé. He's the design guru who founded the hugely successful lifestyle and design magazine *Wallpaper*. He sold it to set up a design consultancy and now flits around the world providing advice wherever it's needed, picking up inspiration and persuading us that makeover is a permanent revolution – though possibly not in exactly the way Marx or Mao had in mind. In his breathless rush between flights, or probably on them, he manages to pen a weekly column for the Saturday *Financial Times* called 'Fast Lane'. He's keen to help us with our lifestyles, but it's not always easy.

I'm occasionally reluctant to reveal some of my favourite venues to eat, drink, shop and sleep on this page. It's not because I don't want to have breakfast with you on a side street in Copenhagen, compete with you for a prime pool position on Lago di Garda or watch you disrobe at an *onsen* outside Nagano. It's because some gems are best left unpolished. There's always a tricky balance between ensuring that a small café in Dornbirn, a kitchen shop in Chur or an *alimentari* in Chiavenna gets enough trade to tick over and pay the bills but not so much celebrity that it suddenly has the funds to renovate and install a cheap and nasty shop fit.

Indeed, indeed. One can perfectly understand his reluctance. One can't have the civilians polishing one's little gems. As for Mr Brûlé's own dream of the ultimate lifestyle, it's this: a little house 'hanging somewhere over Palm Beach' in Australia, where

lots of friends will stop in to detox, refocus and rest.

You get the sort of demographic he mixes with from that one little line. It may possibly explain why, in listing the brands he advised us to have nothing to do with, he took a pot-shot at easyJet (or indeed 'easy-Anything'). It provoked this retort from easyJet's boss, Sir Stelios Haji-Ioannou:

Not everyone can flit around the world like a faded aristocrat cherry-picking preferred upmarket brands and locations.

Which is more or less what you would have expected him to say. But what was interesting (and curiously heartrending) was another response to this little spat from an *FT* reader who said this about Mr Brûlé's lifestyle guidance:

It is a revelation to me every week about brands and service standards that I have not experienced . . . yet.

No knowledge is superfluous, as Dante Alighieri said.

It was the 'yet' that was telling. The writer of the letter, Kenny Muncaster, lives in West Cumbria, one of the poorest areas of Britain and earns forty-five pounds a week delivering newspapers, starting at four fifteen in the morning. He went on:

> I may live in crushing poverty and have existed on a
> sub-standard diet for the past four years. But I know
> quality.

Such is the attraction of lifestyle and the power of fantasy.

Mr Muncaster's predicament does rather bring us back to reality and the challenge of how we are to pay for our chosen lifestyles. Note the word 'challenge'. We must expunge the word 'problem' from our vocabulary for a start. Far too negative. Happily, language comes to the rescue again to show us that it need not be much of a challenge at all.

I refer to the language of those enticing mailshots that pour through our letterboxes. You know them well. We have invariably been 'specially invited' to apply for a loan – but not just any old loan. We are 'a preferred MBNA customer' entitled to a 'Platinum Loan'. Some tell us we have been 'selected' for a loan – unless, importantly, we have been 'pre-selected'. The flattering implication of being pre-selected is slightly undermined by the final sentence inviting you to pass on this amazing offer to a friend if you're not interested. It's not as if the company would lend their money to any old Joe out there. Is it?

It 'couldn't be easier' to get your hands on the cash. A decision on your application can be made 'usually within minutes' and a cheque 'couriered to you within 24 hours'. As for paying interest, you'll enjoy 'a great low rate' – another phrase that's problematic only for the miserably pedantic. The important thing is that you shouldn't worry about any of it. Indeed, you can 'relax with 0% for up to nine months'.

Of course, you might be one of those people who's already stacked up quite a bit of debt. But don't let that disturb you. You can 'consolidate' your debts. Now that's a fine, solid word, is it not? You can convert them all into a single debt. That way you'll be able to 'rearrange your credit into one affordable loan' or end up with 'one low easy rate' to pay.

'Affordable'. 'Low'. 'Easy'. Such reassuring words. And there are others. If you go for a consolidated loan, your debt will be 'secured'. Now, how reassuring is that? So much wiser than, say, 'unsecured', wouldn't you think? Except that it means your debts are, for the first time, secured against your house. So if you don't keep up the payments you could lose the roof over your head. And the payments are 'easy' only in the sense that you have to make one big one rather than several little ones. They are 'affordable' and 'low' only because you're going to be paying them for very much longer.

A small footnote to the search for the elusive new lifestyle that may or may not be connected to the above: for the first time in history, personal debt in this country has passed one trillion pounds. That's an awful lot of noughts. The number of personal bankruptcies was forecast to rise beyond 100,000 in a single year.

If cheap'n'easy debt is not the way for you, there is an alternative route to the lifestyle makeover of your dreams. It was set out in another little leaflet that dropped on to my doormat and was entitled 'Never Stop Dreaming'.

> This week a sports car. Next week a round-the-world cruise. The week after that, how about a luxury villa abroad?

Sounds pretty good to me. The leaflet went on:

> A National Lottery Subscription gives you the chance to dream about ways of spending your winnings every week, because every week like clockwork, we'll enter your numbers into the draw for you.

Put aside any alarm you may feel that anyone would want to take out a subscription to a lottery and admire, for a moment, the clever piece of drafting in that sentence. Taken literally, it's silly: it says that a subscription will give you the 'chance to dream', as if you couldn't dream without a subscription. But, of course, we must not take it literally. The really slick little phrase is:

> the chance to dream about ways of spending your winnings every week.

So you'll be 'spending your winnings every week', will you? There's a problem here. To spend them every week would you not have to win every week? Indeed you would. But it would infringe every advertising law since Moses to guarantee something that is less likely to happen than Ms Hurley becoming a Carmelite nun. Which is why it doesn't actually say it . . . just allows you to think it. The great thing, though, is that a subscription means

> You'll never have to worry about forgetting to buy a Lottery ticket . . .

How wonderful to have the lifting of that particular 'worry'. And it's not the only worry they can help us with:

> . . . Or checking to see whether your numbers have come up. We'll take care of that too.

What nice people they are – and with such a homely, caring way of explaining how automatic computer systems work. All I need do, it seems, is sign on the dotted line – remembering, of course, to print my bank details clearly on the direct debit form – and . . .

. . . that's it. Once you've subscribed, all you have to
do is sit back, relax and start dreaming.

To sit back and relax seems to be the default
position of the fantasy lifestyle we are all being invited
to aspire to. For myself, I feel that if I had sat back and
relaxed as much as I have been encouraged to do over
recent years, I would have become permanently hori-
zontal long ago.

But I have to admit that I am not very good at sitting
back and relaxing. I keep getting bugged by this
thought. Such a posture, though comfortable, is perhaps not the best one for keeping your wits about you
while others 'take care' of your makeover, your lifestyle, your growing debt, gambling habits and anything else they can think of.

You don't suppose that is precisely why they suggest
it, do you?

CHAPTER FIVE

Now Isn't Soon Enough

As you would expect of somebody in my job, I have a great interest in sleep. An obsession with it would be more accurate. When you get up in the middle of the night several times a week, having enough sleep matters a great deal. I always want a little more. Some people feel the same way about food or drink and that, I suppose, is worse. At least sleep is relatively harmless and it's free. But will it stay that way? The *Sunday Times* reported a businessman saying this about snoozing:

> 'a 21st-century luxury which we, as a retailer of sleep, want to sell'.

The speaker was a chap called Wayne Munnelly and he rejoices in the title of director of sleep for Travelodge. So obviously he's got to flog the stuff one way or the other. But Professor Jim Horne doesn't, yet even he talks about sleep in a vaguely commercial manner. He runs the Sleep Research Laboratory at Loughborough University and he's been researching sleep for thirty years. He says there has been more interest in sleep and 'sleep products' in the past five years than in the previous thirty put together. Presumably selling sleep is only the beginning. How long before we learn about the appointment by another big company of a director of breathing? There has to be really, really serious money in retailing breathing, don't you think?

But then I came across an even more alarming headline. It read:

Say Goodbye to Sleep

The story was based on a piece in the *New Scientist* by Graham Lawton about a new drug that can apparently enable us to stay awake for days and get what amounts to a whole night's sleep in just a few hours. Yves, a thirty-one-year-old software developer from Seattle, has tried it:

'If I take a dose just before I go to bed, I can wake up after four or five hours and feel refreshed. I'm more organised and more motivated, and it means I can go out partying on a Friday night and still go skiing early on Saturday morning.'

The drug is called Modafinil and was described by Lawton thus:

a lifestyle drug for people who want off-the-peg wakefulness

That is a masterpiece of the language of consumer choice, each little element doing its bit. And there's our old friend 'lifestyle' again, used so casually in such a matter-of-fact way, with the easy assumption that we lead lifestyles rather than lives and recreational drugs are just a normal part of them.

'Off-the-peg wakefulness' beautifully captures the spirit of the times: the notion that anything we might want should be available instantly on demand. And near the top of any wish-list would be – why not? – a permanent 'wakefulness' that allows us to party all night and play all day.

In some ways, though, the most interesting word in Lawton's marvellous phrase is the most unobtrusive one: 'want'. It is obviously the word at the centre of con-sumerism and carries with it all those feelgood qualities of freedom and choice and liberation: you can decide what you want and, what's more, you can have it. The consumer is sovereign. We make choices. We choose what we want. But with this new medicine things are not quite so simple. As Lawton put it:

> We seem to be moving inescapably towards a society where sleep and wakefulness are available, if not on demand, then at least on request.

It's the 'inescapably' that's a bit troubling. An inexor-able process seems to be under way in which

> . . . we are too far down the road of the 24-hour society to turn back.

So perhaps this is about more than simply 'wanting' – about being able to choose to party all Friday night

99

and go skiing on Saturday morning – which is what the purveyors of 'lifestyle drugs' would have us believe.

The history of this particular drug is instructive. Lawton tells us it was originally developed to help people suffering from Alzheimer's to offset the effects of sleep deprivation. Then its use was extended into providing a 'lifestyle drug' to *facilitate* sleep deprivation among those who want to party and ski as much as they can. What might the next stage be? Once those who burn candles at both ends have set the norm, others may well be *expected* to take the drug to keep up with them. Before long the market for it stretches way beyond any sense of people 'wanting' it to those persuaded they 'need' it.

It is already being looked at closely by the American military. They can see its advantage to soldiers, who have to stay awake for very long stretches on special operations. But remember that we all now live in a twenty-four-hour society. Remember, too, that many people struggle desperately to make ends meet – sometimes because of all that partying and skiing, but sometimes because they don't earn enough to take the kids on a decent holiday once a year or to lead a reasonable life. The more desperate might see the advantage of working far longer hours – possibly even two jobs.

So the next stage could be a transition from 'lifestyle' drug to 'livelihood' drug. Employers might even provide it for free. After all, it's not hard to imagine the argument they'd use to get their workers to take it. It's a tough old world out there. Our twenty-four-hour society has come along at the same time as globalisation. With all those Chinese and Indians beavering away for a pittance, it's hard to stay competitive. Productivity is the answer.

It doesn't take much for the dream of free consumer choice to become the nightmare of necessity.

'Want' is not the only misleadingly simple word in the world of lifestyle consumer choice. Take another we bandy around without thinking about it: 'demand'. It's been part of the furniture since 1776 when Adam Smith tried to get our thinking about economics on to a more organised footing. Supply and demand have been the basis of the dismal science ever since.

The word 'supply' poses no problems: it expresses straightforwardly what producers can provide. But why should the word for what consumers might want be 'demand'? Why should we talk of 'consumer demand' rather than say, 'consumer desire', or 'consumer requirement' or even 'consumer request'? The point about a request is that it can be – and often is – denied. But 'demand' is different.

'Demand' suggests peremptoriness, rude insistence, grabbing rather than trading. It translates into 'gotta have it', the 'must-have handbag' and the clothes that are 'to die for' – though shouldn't that be 'to kill for'?

Above all, the word suggests childishness, the little horror staging a temper tantrum, stamping his feet and demanding he gets what he wants. We train children out of this sort of thing, persuading them that if they ask nicely they're more likely to achieve what they are after. But for some reason adults, as consumers, go on 'demanding'.

Poor Adam Smith didn't have this in mind at all. He was simply using a term that would relate the quantity of a particular product that people might fancy to the price at which they'd be prepared to buy it. There might very well be an infinite 'demand' from children for the latest PlayStation – but if its price is roughly what their grandparents paid for their first house it limits the number bought. Our everyday use of the word 'demand' has rather lost sight of the price bit. The sense is that whatever consumers 'demand' they must have – no argument.

That assumption, conveniently woven into the ordinary meaning of the word, crops up everywhere. The Department of Transport tells us that 'demand for air travel' will increase from 180 million passengers per year to 476 million by 2030. The assumption is that because there is this 'demand' it must be supplied. Another government department tells us we must worry about climate change and everyone knows that air travel is the fastest growing source of carbon-dioxide emissions. But demand is demand is demand – so the new airports will be built and the old runways extended whatever the environmentalists may say.

The real oddity, though, is that we consumers are not as demanding as the word might suggest. Taken to the water, we sometimes have to be made to drink. Otherwise there would be no need for all the advertising to 'create demand' for a product.

This is a phrase that becomes more extraordinary the more you think about it. On one hand you have all the associations of the urgent, the spontaneous, the uncompromising and the insistent resonance of the word 'demand'. On the other, there is the contradictory sense of work and effort, artifice and manipulation going into 'creating' it. When you think about it, it's a glorious oxymoron, on a par with Willie Whitelaw's famous comment about 'stirring up apathy'.

At least, it should be. But we take the idea of creating demand as an unremarkable part of our world. Perhaps it's because we have misunderstood something else. We tend to think of the phrase 'consumer demand' as meaning quite simply the demand of consumers. But maybe the preposition is wrong. Maybe it means the demand *on* consumers: the demand on them to, well, demand.

And, of course, once we've succumbed, the demands really are *on* us because now we must pay. So off we go to earn the money and if we can't earn enough we go into debt or maybe into the warm, dreaming embrace of the National Lottery or even one day – who knows? – into the grip of the off-the-peg-wakefulness drug.

And it really is 'inescapable': we're all in this together. Every economist I know says our relative economic prosperity of the past few years has been built largely on the back of consumer demand and the debt incurred to meet it. If we stop demanding, we're all sunk. Perhaps, in the end, it's just as well we have such a thuggish word to describe what we 'want' to keep the whole thing going.

Those of us in what Shakespeare rather hurtfully described as the seventh age may feel we are now largely exempt from all this. After all, we are not demanding off-the-peg wakefulness: just a bit of it now and again would do very nicely, thank you. As for the twenty-four-hour society, John McEnroe expressed it perfectly: 'You have GOT to be kidding!'

There has been an interesting shift here. Grandparents have always marvelled, with a mixture of pleasure and envy, at the things it's possible for their grandchildren to do but which they could only have dreamed of doing themselves. Now they wonder why anyone would *want* to do them.

Why, they ask, would someone choose to go to what they used to call a nightclub but which now *opens* at nine o'clock on a Sunday morning? Answer: because the demand has been created to go clubbing continuously from Friday night to Monday morning. What's the problem, Grandpa? If you've got the right drugs, lots of bottled water and plenty of readies . . .

An eighty-year-old told me that she hoped she wouldn't live too long because the world was fast becoming more unfamiliar, even more alien, than she could handle. As she put it in a perfectly cheery tone: 'I don't know how to "Visit our Website" and I don't bloody well want to anyway!'

But the elderly should not imagine they are going to be let off the important task of creating demand quite so easily. In the spring of 2006, when many of them may have been pootling around in their greenhouses pricking out the sweet peas, the big retail companies were forking out £700 a ticket to attend a one-day conference in London focused on helping them get their hands into elderly pockets. You can see why they'd want to. The over-fifties control 80 per cent of the UK's wealth, 60 per cent of its savings and 40 per cent of its disposable income. By 2010 they will constitute half of the population. The title of the conference was:

Turning Grey Into Gold: Blending Cutting-Edge Population Knowledge With Innovative Marketing To Segment And Connect With The Older Market.

Pretty punchy, eh? What a joy it is to get back into the language of marketing executives. No, I shan't attempt to decode it (or even 'connect with' it) but one thing is worth noting: the word 'older'. The phrase 'the old' seems to be dying out. Judges are often given guidance on what is called 'inappropriate terminology'. They have been warned off 'old' because it carries connotations of being 'worn out and of little further use'. Well, quite. I recognise the symptoms.

Incidentally, if I had the power to issue guidelines I would decree that any reporter at the BBC (or anywhere else) who refers to old people by their first names should be strung up by their heels. It's not just a gross impertinence, it is deeply patronising. The assumption seems to be that once someone passes a certain age they become a child again and are no longer entitled to 'Mr' or 'Mrs'. When Gordon Brown met that remarkable old man Henry Allingham, the last living survivor of the Battle of Jutland who was celebrating his hundred and tenth birthday, the Chancellor was referred to in several reports as Mr Brown but Mr Allingham became 'Henry'. What a bloody cheek.

Anyway, the advertisement for the marketing conference referred to 'the older audience' and 'the mature consumer'. Best of all it said:

> Leading speakers will deliver insightful case studies
> to propel your brand into the grey limelight.

What an extraordinary use of language that is. 'Grey limelight' is either completely bonkers or a work of marketing genius – though I suppose, in this strange world, it could be both. We would normally associate grey and old (or even 'older') with 'twilight' but here, with just a slight twist, we are invited instead to see the nation's wrinklies kicking up their heels and enjoying the limelight. It's all about feelgood, of course. Pick up any piece of Saga literature and you'll find seventy-year-olds whitewater-rafting or bungee-jumping all over the place. In a world where sixty-year-olds become mothers it's entirely plausible that marketing people should propel their feelgood brands into the grey limelight.

And if feelgood doesn't work in creating demand . . . well, there's always 'feelbad'. That's not in the dictionary because I've just coined it. The most potent feelbad tactic is to persuade us we're suffering from something not far short of an illness. This sort of advertisement, for instance:

> Growing Concerns: 1 in 4 women in the UK suffer from thinning hair

Advertisers love 'suffer'. I'd prefer to save such a powerful word for people with something a bit more serious than thinning hair. Obviously there's no reason why a company should not try to flog us something to help our hair grow back and if it really is one in four there's a massive market out there. But the advertisement implies that this commonplace and harmless condition is tantamount to an illness that needs treating.

It tells us that the effectiveness of the product is 'clinically proven' – just as a medicine has to be – and that it has the potential for 'helping thousands of women'. That's the sort of language that is more legitimately used when medical research comes up with a breakthrough for, say, breast cancer. To steal the words of the advertisement itself, 'feelbad' advertising is 'worrying, upsetting and damages confidence'.

In *Lost for Words* I drew attention to this trick of creating demand by inventing pseudo-illnesses. Some of it is pretty blatant. You take an ordinary condition, tack on the word 'syndrome' and you're away. Some of it is marginally more subtle. In my book I mentioned an advertisement that asked us in a very concerned way whether we showed 'signs of daily fatigue'. There's only one answer to that: who doesn't? But the real answer, we learned, was to take a little capsule and 'say goodbye to daily fatigue'. 'Saying goodbye' seems rather to be in fashion.

Since my book came out academics have got on the case. In early 2006 the journal *Public Library of Science Medicine* published no fewer than eleven learned articles from around the world on what one academic called the 'corporate-sponsored creation of disease' or, for the popular press, 'disease-mongering'.

Iona Heath, a GP in London, was quoted as saying: 'Disease-mongering exploits the deepest atavistic fears of suffering and death. It is in the interests of pharmaceutical companies to extend the range of the abnormal so that the market for treatments is proportionately enlarged.' That's as good a case of 'creating demand' as I know.

The academics talked about the familiar cases, such as diagnosing naughty children with attention deficit hyperactivity disorder, but there were others. There's now something called 'social anxiety disorder', known to you and me as shyness. We're encouraged to wonder whether the mood-swings we all experience from time to time may not really be signs of bi-polar disorder, which can be a truly hellish disease. And then there's 'restless legs syndrome'. You may want to laugh at this – though you wouldn't if you suffered from it – but it's the language used to talk about it that is so revealing. This is how the giant pharmaceutical company, GlaxoSmithKline, puts it:

> It's estimated that 10–15% of adults suffer from restless legs syndrome, yet it is a very underdiagnosed medical condition, which even when diagnosed, often leaves people without effective treatment. About 3% of adults experience moderate to severely distressing RLS symptoms at least two or three times a week and are likely to benefit from treatment.

'Underdiagnosed' is a wonderful new word. I can perfectly well understand 'incorrectly diagnosed'. There was the remarkable case recently of a poor chap called Derek Kirchen who was diagnosed with lung cancer. Doctors were pretty confident that he had a bad tumour. For about eighteen months he'd had endless bouts of pneumonia, kept collapsing and had a seriously worrying lump in his lung. So he was admitted to hospital for an operation. When they inserted a tube, they discovered that the lump was not quite so sinister. It was a cashew nut. Mr Kirchen remembered that the last time he'd eaten one was two Christmases ago and it had 'gone down the wrong way'. When he came round from the operation, he said: 'All the nurses were laughing. They couldn't believe it.' He doesn't even like cashew nuts.

But 'underdiagnosed' is rather more puzzling than 'incorrectly diagnosed'. Presumably it means doctors aren't diagnosing the particular condition often enough – which might possibly suggest that not enough people are complaining about it. And that's a bit odd if they really *are* 'suffering' from it.

The other trick in the marketing books is to create demand by suggesting that a treatment offered for a specific condition suffered by a few might do us all a bit of good. That's the point made by Dr Joel Lexchin, of York University in Toronto, about Viagra and its makers, Pfizer. He alleges that the company has designed ways to 'ensure that the drug was seen as a legitimate therapy for almost any man' and that the message from its ads and website 'is that everyone, whatever their age, at one time or another, can use a little enhancement.'

Pfizer denies it, yet Viagra is increasingly talked about not just as a treatment for a medical condition but as a lifestyle drug. Versions of it are certainly widely available as such. I suppose you could call it a 'lifestyle drug for people who want off-the-peg wakefulness'. Of a sort.

It's certainly one way to say goodbye to sleep.

CHAPTER SIX

Formal Warning

The sociologist Zygmunt Bauman has said that to be a 'successful' consumer now defines what it is to be 'normal'. So it is not surprising to discover how many activities are now seen in consumerist or business terms. A British actor who appears on a Broadway stage is described as a 'talented export'. We no longer watch television news but, in the language of the broadcasting bosses, 'consume' it. The country itself is routinely called 'UK plc' – as though that's all it is. But the winner of gold in this category must be this – from a study commissioned by the United States Army:

> For the army to achieve its mission goals with Future Force Soldiers, it must overhaul its image as well as its product offering.

How much mightier would Churchill's oratory have been in those dark days of 1940 if only Britain had had its own Military Image Study:

> We shall fight on the beaches with our product offering. We shall fight in the hills and the marketing directors' expense-account restaurants. We shall

never surrender in the battle to defend our bottom line. And even if, which I do not for a moment believe, this great company were the target of an unscrupulous takeover bid, then our sales divisions beyond the seas, armed and guarded by our refurbished image and exciting new logo, would carry on the struggle . . . Let us therefore brace ourselves to our duties, and so bear ourselves that, if UK plc last for a thousand focus groups, men will still say, 'This was their finest hour.'

Well, it's not *that* far-fetched when you consider that a British education minister has referred to our universities as 'UK Knowledge plc', which needs to keep up its 'market share'. No less a figure than the Chancellor of Oxford University, Lord Patten, has spoken about his ancient institution as being part of 'the global university market', needing to 'trawl the world for the best students'.

I know that universities need to raise money wherever they can but using language like this has consequences. It's not surprising if students come to see themselves more as customers than as members of their universities. In one sense they are: they have to pay and they want value for money. Why not? But it seems that increasing numbers of them interpret that in the ordinary sense of customers' rights.

They're encouraged in that by marketing slogans such as:

Personalising your journey

That's ideal, you may think, for an upmarket travel agency offering two weeks' hiking in the Himalayas. But I'm told this is what students are to be offered at university. A friend runs a consultancy whose clients include some of our newer universities – the ones we called polytechnics not so long ago. He is being paid to advise them on how best to enrich the 'student experience' by 'personalising the journey'. If you are baffled by this language, don't fret. So is he.

The travel agency comparison turns out to be close to the mark. Baroness Deech is the first independent adjudicator for Britain's university sector and it has been an eye-opener for her:

> 'When I first started this job, somebody said education was like going on holiday – you get your glossy prospectus, pay your money and if there are cockroaches in the hotel you sue.'

In other words the attitude of some students was: 'I've paid my money and I've got to get an upper second and it's the university's job to make sure I do. I'm the customer, remember.' But it doesn't (and obviously shouldn't) work quite like that. Customers are frequently disappointed. When that happens in the world of commerce they complain. And that's exactly what they are doing now in academe. There were five times as many complaints from students in 2005 as there had been in 2004 and many of them, it seems, expressed in language you might use to complain about a rip-off merchant. Lady Deech was not impressed:

'In the course of looking at some complaints, we have seen emails from students to tutors which astonish me.'

Another effect of the tendency to interpret all our relationships with each other in commercial terms is that the language in which the 'supplier' speaks to us is changing. It is increasingly rare to come across straightforward statements that convey simple information in a purely formal way. Take this, for example:

To ensure the ongoing quality of your swimming experience, the Club's swimming pool will be closed for annual maintenance from 3 April.

The club in question is the London Central YMCA and that notice appeared in the gym early in 2006. This is what the notice would once have said:

The Club's swimming pool will be closed for annual maintenance from 3 April.

What's wrong with that? It tells the members what is going to happen and why. They will understand perfectly well that swimming pools need regular maintenance. But in this new relationship they must be dealt with as 'customers' so must be subjected to this nonsense. And the language is not only nonsensical, it's hideous.

'Ongoing quality' is entirely vacuous. Does anyone imagine that the people who run the pool would be happy for it to be nice and clean this week and filled with disgusting germs next week?

'Your' is once again meant to reinforce the idea that you personally are at the centre of their universe – in the same way that supermarkets stick up notices talking about 'your' store manager. He's not yours; he's theirs. Try getting him sacked because 'your' store is a mess.

As for 'swimming experience', it is an offence against the English language. In what sense is it an improvement on 'swim'? But then, we have 'reading experiences' these days instead of 'books' so I suppose we shouldn't be surprised. The education minister David Lammy gave an interview to the *Bookseller* magazine in which he said books are 'absolutely essential to the library experience'. Quite so. He should go far.

Does this silly language do any good? Of course not. That's partly because it inspires ridicule but it can also generate suspicion. Language so remote from the way we speak in the real world prompts the question: what's behind all that, then?

Gushing vacuity addressed to customers can have the same effect as excessive flattery: what's he *after*? When we're stuck on the end of a phone and the mechanical voice is saying, for the umpteenth time,

'Your call *is* important to us,' we know that it obviously isn't or they wouldn't have kept us waiting for half an hour and driven us to the edge of insanity with their ghastly Muzak. But sometimes it really *is* valuable to them. Literally. And that's even worse.

In 2005 we spent £1.6 billion dialling premium-rate phone numbers. That's more than any other country in the world – equivalent to thirty-five pounds for every adult – and I'd love to know how much of that is racked up while the mechanical voice tells us how valuable our call is.

On the other hand, at least you don't have to respond to the mechanical voice . . . not the way you do when you get a real person cold-calling on the phone. I had a call the other day from a chap at the *Sunday Times* Wine Club whose opening line was:

'I bet you weren't expecting this call!'

Good God, I thought, it must be Tony Blair offering to confess live on the *Today* programme tomorrow morning that he'd been wrong all the time about Iraq, or maybe the National Lottery telling me I'd won the jackpot – which would indeed have been a great surprise because I have never bought a ticket. Sadly, no. But the cold-callers usually start with:

'I hope I'm not disturbing you.'

How do they expect us to respond to that? 'Disturbing me? Of course not! In fact, I've been sitting by the phone for several days now waiting for someone to call and sell me life insurance I don't want and a new kitchen I don't need to fit into the house with double-glazing that I need even less. So *please* go ahead because I have absolutely nothing better to do than talk to you, and when this call has finished my life will be so empty I shall probably blow my brains out!'

Still, credit where credit's due. At least there is a certain courteous formality in the remark about my being disturbed – and formality matters. It can create a space between us that allows for a measure of independence and freedom. Take it away and that space is open to all manner of intruders, not all of them commercial. When, for example, did you last hear a public figure 'send their condolences' to someone who'd been bereaved? Not recently, I suspect. Nowadays, if there has been a disaster of some sort, it tends to be:

'Our thoughts go out to the loved ones . . .'

Or even:

'All our thoughts are with the families of those . . .'

It may be well meant, but it has the smack of insincerity about it – for the obvious reason that it's not true. 'All' our thoughts do not 'go out' to anyone. Of course all of us will feel a degree of sympathy, but for a

119

politician to suggest that he is thinking of little else is patently false. And it can actually be insensitive to the people who have been bereaved. It is the equivalent of that ghastly and much parodied 'I feel your pain'. The truth is that no one can feel the pain or truly share the suffering of someone who has lost a child, parent or close friend. No one can feel someone else's pain. That's one reason why the pain is so hard to bear: it cannot be shared.

The difference between the old and the new way of expressing sympathy is a clear illustration of how changing language reveals something of the changing nature of our times. The old, formal expression of condolence was just that: the gesture was made and the bereaved were left to their grieving. The new, informal, supposedly more intimate expression pushes the person 'sharing the pain' into the centre of the picture. It sends a message about what *he* is experiencing. It tells us how *he* has been (or claims to have been) affected. No wonder a company's PR department always tells the boss, when disaster strikes, to use the less formal and more intimate language. It deflects criticism and blame by implying that the boss is suffering too – so let's go easy on him.

The new, enforced intimacy is everywhere. The Queen – widely admired for keeping her distance and exercising iron control over her emotions – is now expected to show she cares. It seems a bit odd. Does anyone really believe she somehow became a different person when she was put under pressure to let us know publicly that she was moved by the death of the Princess of Wales?

Formality is disappearing, too, in how we address each other. I knew a young woman in the sixties who got a job as secretary to the headmaster of a public school. After a week or so he said to her: 'Oh, Diana, you really don't need to call me "Sir". Just call me "Headmaster".' At the time we thought it comically stuffy. But that was before a British prime minister encouraged everyone to call him by his Christian name.

The first time I met Tony Blair after the election of 1997 I asked him off-air what I should call him. 'Tony, of course,' he said. I suppose I knew that's what he would say – we'd known each other for a long time and were obviously on first-name terms – but there's something different about being prime minister. It is, when all's said and done, the highest elected office in the land and deserves a special kind of respect. I once toyed with using Margaret Thatcher's first name when she was at Number Ten, but I chose life instead.

On one level this is trivial stuff, but it can matter. Old-fashioned civil servants have always wanted to keep at arm's length from their political bosses. They don't much like first names or approve of chats on sofas and prefer formal meetings around tables with officials present to take notes. There's a reason for that. Running a government is different from organising a village fête. Formality is linked to propriety and propriety is about doing things properly.

It's clear that a lot of the public value old-fashioned formality in the way we talk to each other. If I had a pound for every listener who gets het up when politicians use the interviewer's first name I'd be almost as rich as Terry Wogan or Jonathan Ross. People hate it, so why do the politicians do it? Well, the first thing to be said is that they are not all guilty. Margaret Thatcher never did it. Indeed, in one famous interview with the late Robin Day she called him 'Mr Day' throughout. Which would have been fine – except that he was 'Sir Robin' by that stage in his illustrious career.

Nor does it gain politicians any advantage when they pepper interviews with 'John' or 'Jim'. If they expect us to react like puppies having our tummies tickled . . . well, you'd have thought they might have learned by now that it doesn't work like that. Or maybe they expect us to respond in kind and use their first names too, thus giving the audience the impression that we're all friends together and it's really just a game. That isn't going to happen either. Any political interviewer on a serious programme who calls the politician by his first name should be drummed out of the Brownies. We should keep our distance. Formality is one way of doing so.

But there's an oddity about people's attitude to formality. You know what drives many Radio 4 listeners up the wall? Courtesy. Or, rather, too much of it. This is a common complaint:

The thing I find most annoying is the way you are all constantly thanking each other. For what? Doing your job?

It's difficult to argue with that. On my own programme you might very well hear Greg Wood thanking a guest on his business slot and handing over to me. I thank Greg and hand over to Gary or Steve for the sport and they thank me and then they thank whoever is the guest on their slot, at the end of which they hand back to me and I thank them and . . . well, you get the idea. But what's to be done about it? Yes, I know we're all being paid for what we do and, strictly speaking, there's no need to thank each other. But think about it for a moment.

The waitress is getting paid to bring you your meal in the restaurant, but I bet you thank her anyway. And don't you say, 'Thanks,' when you're handed something in a shop or the hairdresser trims your locks – even though you're paying for the service? And anyway, on programmes such as *Today* you have to end the interviews with *something* – even if it's been just a brief chat with one of your own correspondents.

Indeed, there are occasions when we cut off the thank-you and we shouldn't. The interviewer may have gone ten bruising rounds with a politician who has flatly refused to answer anything except name, rank and serial number. At the end of it the interviewer will say, through gritted teeth: 'Minister, *thank* you!' The minister's response will often be cut off by the studio manager, the person in charge of the technical end of things. I'd prefer to hear it. You can learn a lot from the way the minister responds. A cheery 'Thanks, John' tells you one thing; a snarl tells you something else. But in general there's no question that we overdo our thank-yous.

So it's not like the absurdity of those signposts that pepper our country roads with this message:

'Thank you for driving safely through . . .'

How do they know we were driving safely through their village? And if we were, it would be either because we had nine points on our licence and were terrified of speed cameras lurking behind laurel hedges or because we didn't want to smash into that huge tractor coming around the bend in the opposite direction. In either case, what was there to thank us for? And what if we're so busy reading the signpost that we drive slap bang into the village bobby? Not that there are any village bobbies any longer, so that's alright.

How formal the BBC should be is a controversial issue. Very few people want to return to the days when all announcers had to speak like the Queen, and the idea that the BBC should sound like one small middle-class corner of the south-east of England is preposterous. But there's a powerful argument for some of the formality that has been lost. On the old Third Programme it seldom got much more exciting than an announcer like Patricia Hughes intoning: 'It is ten past four and there now follows a recital of Czech part songs . . .'

You don't get more formal than that. What's interesting about this sort of delivery is that the listener had not the first idea what the announcer thought of the music that was about to be played. She might have considered it the most dreadful old cobblers and couldn't wait to rip off her headphones and nip into the studio next door for a bit of Sinatra. Or she might have sat there enraptured throughout. We had no way of knowing. She left it up to us to decide whether we wanted to hear Czech part songs and, having done so, to decide for ourselves whether it was a good performance or a wretched one. Now we are almost always told how marvellous it all was.

But it's probably the weather forecast that stirs the strongest passion in the breast of the Radio 4 listener. Many mourn the passing of the days when the weather was given straight – even if they had only the vaguest idea why areas of high pressure were a good thing.

A friend was telling me about his childhood holidays in North Wales in the early 1960s. You never knew whether you'd be stuck in the cottage all day, doing jigsaws and watching the rain, or paddling in the surf getting your neck burned red. So you needed to hear the forecast. Just before six every evening, he told me, his father would sternly call for silence. The wireless set would be turned on and a hush would descend on the room as the forecast was delivered. This was a serious business, make no mistake about it, and the seriousness was evident in the formal way the forecast was written. Today it is invariably cheery and chatty and don't forget to take your brolly or pack the sun cream.

You either like it or you loathe it. One listener told me that when he watches certain forecasters on television he immediately finds himself transported back to primary school where he is sitting in the presence of a smiling, reassuring and rather bossy young teacher. Whatever the detail, he says, this is what he actually hears:

> Well, it's going to rain, children, and we don't like rain, do we? But we've got to have it because it's good for us, haven't we? So let's all try to be a little bit grown-up and put a brave face on it. And, of course, we must remember to have our macs with us, mustn't we? And then, who knows?, the day after tomorrow the sun may shine on us all again. Now, I want to see a big smile from everyone . . . George, don't do that . . .

Some people find the formality of the hourly news bulletins, beautifully read by the likes of Harriet Cass and Charlotte Green, too sharp a contrast with the informality of the programmes in which they sit. But I suppose the biggest change has been in the way programmes are trailed and promoted on television. The purpose has always been the same – to encourage us to watch – but the old way was to deliver the information and leave it at that. It seemed almost a matter of indifference to the announcer as to what we did with it. Now the 'promo' is an art form. Cynics say that more effort goes into producing it than into the programme it promotes. And the announcer who does the voice-over bears about as much resemblance to Patricia Hughes as Mike Tyson to Mother Teresa.

On one level the reason for this is obvious: competition. Listeners and viewers have to be fought for. They cannot be taken for granted in the way they were when cable and satellite stations weren't even a gleam in Rupert Murdoch's eye and we could choose any radio station we wanted so long as it was the BBC. But the other reason is the death of formality. One might have expected – or even hoped – that the void would be filled with spontaneity. Instead, in this harsher commercial world, we have the hard sell: manipulative language delivered in slick, sleek packages that tell us we'd be mugs not to buy them.

Tate Modern is a wonderful art gallery – spoiled only by the banality of much of its content. But the building is magnificent and the view of St Paul's across the

Thames is stunning. Tate Britain is another kettle of fish. The Turners alone make it worth a daily visit. But the gallery does not have enough visitors and the people who run it have tried a fresh approach to attract more of us. They've produced new guides – booklets to tell visitors what to expect.

These are not the conventional, formal little guides that provide maps letting you know that the William Blakes are in Room X and the Stanley Spencers in Room Y. Rather, they're leaflets with a marketing spin. The particular sales pitch is to tell you that whatever your current preoccupations, whatever it is that's troubling you or affecting your mood, there's something in the gallery to help. The leaflets identify the pictures you need to look at and where to find them, and the curators have written brief helpful explanations of why particular pictures will do the business.

So, there's one leaflet entitled 'The Calming Collection', one 'The First Date Collection', one 'The Happily Depressed Collection' and one 'The I've Just Split Up Collection'. There are lots of others. The one that caught my eye is called 'The I Have a Big Meeting Collection'. Here's what it says:

> For maximum effect we recommend you experience
> this Collection twenty-four hours prior to a meeting.
> Whatever the reasons for your meeting, we are here
> to help you look good and to ooze confidence. Let's

start by putting you in the mood. Look at *Harvest Home* by John Linnell (room 7). You can almost breathe the fresh air from that golden afternoon. Fill your lungs with greatness. (Always make yourselves bigger before entering a room.)

So *that*'s what Tate Britain is there for – to help me ooze confidence! This is better than assertiveness training. And it's free. There's more:

It's time to take a look at the champion Greek archer *Teucer* by Sir Hamo Thornycroft near the Millbank entrance. He's one of the heroes of Homer's Trojan War. The tip here is never to lose focus on what you're aiming for. You may meditate on this last point over a coffee in the Café.

Ah, yes, the café: the most important place in any museum or gallery. Pictures are free but coffees are a couple of quid. And you can relax. Have a nice time. Watch the world go by . . . But I'm almost forgetting my big meeting.

Now we need to work on your look. Eyes are the most powerful weapons in meetings. Look at *Queen Elizabeth I* (room 2). Study her eyes and her pose. She's the model to follow.

Of course! That's why this is such a great picture. It'll help me to storm into a meeting tomorrow with the BBC Director-General, eyes blazing, looking like

Gloriana (only bigger – remember the first lesson). But we're not finished yet.

> With just a glance at *The Fisherman's Farewell* (room 21) you'll see a man saying goodbye to his family. But if you look deeper, you'll find determination and character. You should look like him by now.

Funny that. This painting strikes many people as being about anxiety and the reluctance to part, about the grinding necessity of earning a living and about the terrible fear of loss that's at the heart of love. But obviously we should look 'deeper' (or possibly even 'more deeply').

> Finally, spend some time in front of *The Battle of Camperdown* (room 9) – meetings are often like that. No one said it was going to be easy. But the painting still depicts the moment of victory. Bravery is the name of the game. Off you go.

Off I go indeed. This has really set me up. I'm a different person. By now I'm striding purposefully out of the gallery, resisting distraction from mere art to the left and right of me and probably already on my mobile barking new instructions to my secretary. Now I understand why we subsidise the arts.

But let's try to be generous to the sophisticated nabobs who run the Tate. Let's suppose they're just having a bit of fun – messing about with the notion of the post-modern, where texts both do and don't mean what they say. Maybe. Or maybe they're ticking boxes for bureaucrats. The people who dole out the cash have no doubt told the gallery that they must get visitor numbers up. They must increase 'accessibility'. They must make it all much more 'user-friendly'. They must make it fun. They must make it easy.

So, things have had to change at Tate Britain. Under the old formality, a gallery said in a neutral sort of way: 'Here we are. Here are some paintings. Come and look at them if you'd like to. Make of them what you will . . .' But that won't do any longer. The targets, God forbid, might not be met. So the calm, neutral space that was once created by the inexpressive formality of a gallery must now be filled with spin and salesmanship. We must be sold the line that art is 'relevant' to us. It's there to serve our needs. And there's not a single need, however trivial or mundane, to which it cannot cater. There's even the 'I'm Hungover Collection', if that's your problem.

You wanted to know what the purpose of art is? It's obvious. It exists to help us all perform better and make life easier. You can almost hear a junior minister in the Department of Culture, Media and Sport making a speech about it:

'This has got to be good for everyone. It's good for individuals – people need help and it's our duty to provide it. It's good for the galleries – they don't want to stay as fuddy-duddy institutions no one visits. They want to move with the times. And, above all, it's good for Britain. Don't forget – those big meetings really do matter. It's a tough world out there. If we're going to stay competitive in a global-ised economy, everyone's got to be able to perform at the top of their game. If the art world can help us do that, then it's a win-win situation!'

The only trouble with all this is that it destroys art in the process. It's what Marxists would call the 'com-modification of art'.

My own vague, tentative, no doubt ill-informed notion of what art might be derives from the ex-perience of seeing something, or reading it, or hear-ing it and feeling as if I'm being removed from the familiar clutter and preoccupations of my life. The effect of art is to take us out of ourselves, to transport us from the insistent parochialism of our daily existence. The experience may not always be comfortable or easy – even with a coffee thrown in. It may be disturbing, shaking the complacency with which we tend to see the world as a reflection of our own purposes and selfish little interests. If we deprive art of the neutral, unspun way it comes to us and instead recruit it as servant to those purposes, we destroy its power.

Those little leaflets remind me of the old cartoon of a flustered woman rushing into the Louvre and shouting at a startled attendant: 'Where's the Mona Lisa? I'm double-parked!'

What is revealing about the language of the Tate's leaflets is not that it's used to bamboozle us in the way a gallery of contemporary art might – and try to con us into believing that it is we who are at fault if we cannot see why a video 'installation', for instance, is truly a piece of art. It's the opposite. It seems designed to get us to overlook the fact that these paintings are great works of art and tells us instead that we can enlist them to serve our blinkered lives. But their glory lies precisely in their being able to take away those blinkers.

Formality may seem stuffy but it provides fresh air and freedom compared with this.

CHAPTER SEVEN

The Word on the Street

It really is true that there's no fool like an old fool. I have been a journalist for almost half a century – in broadcasting for most of that time – and I am living proof of it. I have delivered a lecture, engaged in debates and written several lengthy articles about the vacuous nature of much modern television – above all, the monstrous confidence trick that goes by the name of 'reality television'.

I do not deny that some of it is hugely entertaining. Indeed, one or two programmes have been superb. *Operatunity* was television at its best: deeply moving and utterly enthralling. It worked because there was no pretence: it *was* reality. *The Apprentice* and *Dragons' Den* work for the same reason. But most 'reality' television is a lie. It tries to create the illusion that we are watching, people behaving naturally in what are grotesquely contrived circumstances. Anyone who's been in television for five minutes knows that the camera changes everything. Here's how Tom Mangold, one of *Panorama*'s finest reporters, puts it:

'As one who's spent a lifetime being filmed, I promise you I only have to see a camera being unloaded
from a car and I pull my stomach in, adjust my
clothes and wipe my sweaty face. So does everyone
else.'

Indeed we do. Using a word like 'reality' to describe
something that is patently the opposite makes fools of
us all – and worse. The frightfully smart media types
who peddle rubbish like *Big Brother* (and who would
no more dream of appearing on it than they would
sacrifice their first-born) call people like me snobs.
The defence of the programme lies in the size of its
audience, they say. How can the masses be so wrong?
And, anyway, no one really buys into it: they know it's
just a game and they're in on the joke. Sure they are.

So what do I do when the call comes to take part in
a 'reality' show? Like a gullible teenager with stars in
his eyes and mush where his brain should be, I fall for
it. It's true that I had said no to lots of other shows. I
said no to *Big Brother* when I was invited some years
ago to enter the 'celebrity' house – partly on the
Groucho Marx grounds that I would never join any
'celebrity' group that would have me as a member. I
also said no to a spell in the Australian rainforest. So
far, so good. I was still a reality-TV virgin. Then I got
a call wondering if I'd like to take part in a new
programme for BBC2. The idea was that four 'famous'
people (how casually we throw around that word)

would spend a fortnight at the Chelsea Art College being taught how to draw and paint. At the end of the fortnight the work they produced would be exhibited and reviewed by distinguished art critics.

The working title of the programme should have alerted me immediately: *Celebrity Art School*. But I loved the idea. Like half of the population, I can barely draw a bath and I've always wondered whether that's because I was never taught properly. Maybe with a bit of expert tuition I could even sketch a dinosaur that does not resemble a nuclear explosion with a tail. It is deeply hurtful when a very small child looks at you with pity in his eyes and tells you how much better someone else's father is at drawing dinosaurs.

I began to get seriously suspicious, though, when I discovered which production company was making the programme: Endemol. That is the company (the very rich company) that came up with the idea for *Big Brother*. So I said no. Then the phone calls started. A stream of frightfully important people began ringing to persuade me that, no, of course this wasn't going to be some tacky reality-television exercise. But what about Endemol? Ah, this was Endemol *West* – an altogether more upmarket version of the parent company. So that seemed all right, then, and I eventually said yes. But it wasn't all right, and I realised from the first hour of the first day what an idiot I'd been.

The cameras followed us everywhere – not just in the art room but even when we were eating. At least, they did until I told them to clear off. And eventually – just as the producers had hoped and just as I should have grasped if I'd had even half a functioning brain – I lost my temper. I got angry with the producers, angry with the tutors (not that it was their fault) and angry with myself. It made 'good television', of course – which was the whole point. I've no doubt that if live cameras were filming the Second Coming and the Son of God decided to destroy, say, Manchester to teach us all a lesson, the producer would say: 'Shame about Manchester, but it was great television.'

So my tantrums made good television. They also made me look a fool. The *Observer*'s television critic said that if he ever found himself sitting next to me at a dinner party he would probably drive a fork through my hand. And I don't think he was joking.

And yet, in spite of everything, some good came of it. The other 'students' (Clarissa Dickson-Wright, Ulrika Jonsson, Keith Allen and the Radio 1 DJ Nihal) turned out to be great company and we all got on terribly well together – rather to the chagrin, I suspect, of the presenter who tried to entice us into being bitchy about each other. That makes better telly, you understand. But we did not oblige. I also learned a lot about language. It turns out, for example, that 'drawing' no longer means what it once did and neither, for that matter, does 'art'. The word survives but the meaning has been transformed.

Of course art has changed through the ages. Had it not, we'd have been denied the vision of the Impressionists or the radicalism of Picasso – not to mention the nonsense of Tracey Emin and the crude vulgarity of the Chapman brothers. Some of it has added to the gaiety of the nation. You'd have needed a heart of stone not to smile at the man who paid £6.5 million for the famous pickled shark, only to watch it rot gently away before his eyes. There's talk of replacing it with a fresher one – but would it still have the integrity of the original? The worry keeps me awake at night.

Whether or not we still have a firm grasp on the meaning of the word 'art' was a question raised too by the case of the sculptor David Hensel. He made a piece called *One Day Closer to Paradise* of a human head frozen in laughter and balancing precariously on a slate plinth. He submitted it to the Royal Academy for its 2006 Summer Exhibition. Somehow the head and the plinth got separated in transit. Nonetheless the Academy accepted his submission and displayed it. The strange thing was, though, that they thought the plinth was the work of art not the head, which was nowhere to be seen. As he put it ruefully: 'I've seen the funny side but I've also seen the philosophical side . . . It shows up not just the tastes of the selectors but also their unawareness.'

Yet, it's hard not to be impressed by the sheer marketing genius that lies behind contemporary art. Damien Hirst may or may not be the greatest artist of all time but he is, by a country mile, the richest. And Charles Saatchi hasn't done too badly out of it either.

I did not go to art school expecting great riches. I just wanted to learn a little. Indeed, I'd have been quite happy to spend the fortnight doing nothing else. I was even prepared to work hard at it, inspired by no less a figure than Leonardo da Vinci: 'Many are desirous of learning to draw and are very fond of it who are, notwithstanding, void of a proper disposition for it. This may be known by their want of perseverance.' Len, my boy, you said a mouthful there.

I was fully prepared to persevere – but my perseverance was never called for because technique was never called for. The first time I mentioned the word (in about the first hour, as I recall) I was met with an amused tolerance. Poor chap, you could see them thinking, he really is *very* naïve. By the tenth time the tutors were becoming a little irritated. Look, they said, this art thing isn't about learning technique. Sorry, I said, so what *is* it about? And that's the point at which the language became really interesting. It seems it is about the 'concept'. I thought I knew a little about conceptual art – not that I've ever been much impressed by it, but some of it does get you thinking. My problem was that I had failed to think deeply enough.

G. K. Chesterton said that when a man stops believing in God he doesn't then believe in nothing:

he believes in anything. He might have applied that to conceptual art. What I 'learned' during my fortnight at art school was that anything – and, yes, I do mean anything – can be art. And so can nothing. The concept is all. If the artist has a concept but is unable to execute it because he lacks the technique (or gets someone else to do it for him) might he still be a good artist? Yes indeed, they told me. In fact, the ultimate expression of 'conceptual art' is that the 'concept' remains just that: a concept. It is never executed. Yet it is art.

I was informed by the famous art critic who was wheeled in every evening to review our day's 'work' that anybody who couldn't see the artistic integrity in, say, an old bucket was stupid. That exchange came after the business with the mattress. Ulrika and I had been given a carving knife, a pumpkin and an old mattress to create a work of art. By that stage in the proceedings I was beyond boredom, so I vented some of my frustration by sticking the knife into the mattress. Our critic was mightily impressed. I had, it seems, 'brought out the mattressiness' of the mattress. Yes, really. I told her I thought that was ridiculous and she told me I was ridiculous for failing to appreciate my latent genius – which more or less sums up the intellectual level of our exchanges.

As it happens, there was an exhibition of work by Stubbs showing in London at the time. I ventured the opinion that he was rather good – not least because his horses actually looked like horses and came to life on the canvas. Her scorn could have melted tungsten. Didn't I know that things had 'moved on' since Stubbs?

A wonderful phrase that. 'Moved on' – when it comes from the mouths of highly knowledgeable but daft critics – invariably means the opposite of what is intended. Art may well have 'moved on' but only in the sense that Dan Brown with a word-processor has 'moved on' from Shakespeare with his quill pen.

I have always assumed that a work of art must be able to speak for itself. When Jane Austen wrote *Pride and Prejudice* she did not spend the first few pages telling us how funny it was going to be, and when Michelangelo created the *Pietà* he didn't warn us that we might be moved to tears by its beauty and simplicity. Nor did Mozart and Beethoven provide sleeve notes. They created the work and we judged it for ourselves. It doesn't work like that with conceptual art. We are told why the artist is so very, very clever and what he or she had in mind with this particular piece of genius. No doubt that's intended to pre-empt any notion that the emperor has no clothes.

It's always interesting to compare what happens in an exhibition of, say, the Impressionists and one of our great contemporary artists. When people approach a Monet they will stand and look at the picture – often for quite a long time. Then they might look at the notes, if any are provided. When they approach a Hirst or an Emin they will do things in reverse. The truly sophisticated will nod sagely – especially if they think they are being watched. The rest will look baffled and move on to the next piece of blurb. When my mutilated mattress is finally exhibited at Tate Modern I shall insist on its mattressiness being explained in great detail.

So it became clear pretty quickly that I was not going to learn what I'd come for and that, like the naughty boy in the class, I'd get more out of messing about with the other kids than from what Teacher might have to say. Fortunately, as I say, the 'other kids' were great.

At first Nihal and I were slightly wary of each other. I suspect he thought I was a boring old hack obsessed with politics who knew nothing about modern music and cared even less. He was right about that last bit. What was more, I had not the vaguest idea how people like him earned their keep. I have never quite seen the point of DJs or understood why the best of them are more famous (and often richer) than the bands whose work they play. He set me straight on all that. He also taught me a lot about language.

Radio 4 presenters are expected to conform to certain norms, to speak a language with which the audience is comfortable. Nihal is under just as much pressure from his audience to challenge the norms. A Radio 1 DJ who does not speak the language of his (mostly) young listeners will soon be shown the door.

We made up our own language at school – mostly in the hope that the grown-ups wouldn't know what we were talking about. It seldom worked, but it does today. A teenager will use words that are often incomprehensible to his parents or mean the precise opposite of what they assume. And the language will be heavily influenced by other cultures and the all-pervasive rap.

I wondered if an ageing Radio 4 presenter could learn 'street' – not that I'd ever try to speak it, obviously. In one of his masterly *Letters from America* Alistair Cooke used a lovely expression to describe something un-seemly. It was, he said, like nudging a pretty girl at a funeral. That applies to anyone over a certain age trying to sound like someone a generation younger. But Nihal humoured me and gave me a lesson.

He was good at it – and he has the most extra-ordinary talent for rap. You give him a subject – just about anything that comes into your mind – and in a couple of minutes he's off. I may not be one of nature's natural rappers, but I flatter myself that I have a reasonably good ear for language. I reckoned I could get away with a bit of 'Hey, man . . . how ya doin'?' and 'Know what I'm sayin'?' and using 'cool' at every opportunity rather than 'That's fine'. But, no, it doesn't work like that. Street language is inventive and rich.

I tried to imagine myself as a hip young dude meeting my equally cool young friend on the street.

(Yes, I know, you'll need a lot of imagination for this.) How would he greet me? Would we have to high-five each other? What would he say? Rather disconcertingly, Nihal told me, he might very well say nothing. There would be lots of touching fists, handshakes, hugs . . . very tactile (though only between men). It's part of being down.

'Being down'? I'd heard of 'being up'. One of the 2006 *Big Brother* saddos (a serious insult when used by one teenager about another) talked a lot about wanting to 'have it up, big time'. Or even: 'I like to go out there and blaze it up. I just like to have everyone up, everything, d'you get me?' Not really, to be honest, but Nihal had this explanation for 'being down':

> 'It's about being part of something. It's like being real. *You* understand where *I*'m coming from; *I* understand where *you*'re coming from. So it's like Freemasons: they have handshakes showing 'I'm down with you and you're down with me.' We're part of that thing. If you break something down you're getting to the essence of something. Being down is being at the essence of something.'

So what happens after the fist-touching and hugging? Not a lot, says Nihal: 'There's a million ways of not saying anything. Two people could walk up and say: "What's happenin'? Cool, man. What's goin' on with you? Good? All good? Things are runnin'? Peace. Safe."'

'Peace' means 'I'm outa here' (it's a long story) and 'safe' means 'We're safe with each other'; there's no animosity. The idea of things runnin' originates in Jamaica. A Jamaican who says, 'Big tings are gwang,' means: 'I've got lots of things running through my life at the moment . . . a lot of big projects going on.'

There is a well-known dark side to contemporary street rap. An alarming number of the words used to describe a woman imply that she is the property of her man, to treat as the mood takes him. And women are denigrated routinely. 'Bitch' is used for girlfriend and 'sket' is a loose woman. This is from NWA's Ice Cube:

Do I look like a mothafuckin' role model?
To a kid lookin' up ta me
Life ain't nothin' but bitches and money.

'Gangsta' rap has been around for nearly twenty years and it's pretty frightening. It's impossible to be sure, as David Cameron believes, that lyrics glorifying violence encourage people to carry guns and knives. It's obvious, though, that the genre has influenced fashion. The reason youngsters wear their trousers slung so low that the crotch is around the knees is because American convicts are not issued with belts.

Not that rap sanctions any language, however offensive. You would not, for instance, call someone a 'nigger'. Or at least, according to the subtleties revealed by my tutor Nihal, not unless you were careful how you spelled it. He explained that the word has been reclaimed by Afro-Americans. The film *Deep Cover* begins with a white cop asking a black cop about the 'difference between a black man and a nigger'. Eventually the black cop says the difference is that 'Only a nigger would answer the question.'

Here's how Nihal put it: 'If you spell it N-I-G-G-E-R, that's derogatory; if you spell it N-I-G-G-A . . . that's my boy; that's my friend! In America you have the phenomenon where nigga becomes just "friend".' I asked Nihal, who's Asian, if he would use it and he said he would not because he's slightly older. 'Those guys who use it (the ones in their twenties), they were never chased down the street by skinheads. They missed out on that. I didn't miss out on it.'

But he does use 'Paki' or 'TP' (typical Paki): 'If you're two hours late for a meeting, that's TP. I'd probably say that. It would be ironic, never with hatred or anger. It's like saying "idiot". A young Asian wouldn't be offended.'

This sort of language, though, treads on very thin ice. Chris Moyles, Radio 1's most famous DJ, got into a lot of bother when he described on air someone's ring-tone as 'gay'. He meant that it was rubbish. Does that mean gays are rubbish? Well, no. It's just that the word 'gay' has come to mean 'lame' or 'rubbish' among a certain group of young people. Even the BBC governors adjudicated that the word was in 'widespread current usage' in this harmless and in-offensive way among the young and that Moyles was only reflecting the fact. But that didn't stop some people complaining. They argued that for anyone from the BBC to use the term like this was 'cruel and scarring' for homosexuals. Funny how one little word can mean 'full of or disposed to joy and mirth', 'homosexual' and 'rubbish'. It just shows that context is everything.

Nihal told me that if you really do want to insult someone in 'street' you might call him 'chief'. No one seems quite sure why.

The point of this intriguing language, according to Nihal, is 'to separate me from you'. He says: 'It's like Latin in the Church. Knowledge is power. I've got knowledge on the street. That separates me from my parents. For example, I could be talking to my boys on the phone and saying, "I'm shifting keys at the moment. I've got some green coming in." That's talking about drugs. Keys equals kilos; green equals weed. If you said, "We were blazing hard the other night," you'd mean you were smoking lots of weed. If your parents heard you they wouldn't know what you were talking about.'

In fact, the moment older people *do* know is the moment the language dies. 'Bling' is a classic example, says Nihal: 'As soon as you hear commissioning editors at Channel 4 using it you know it's dead. Ali G killed off a lot of language. His creator was a nice, Cambridge-educated Jewish boy and he was taking the piss out of the way people speak. It was deadly.'

So who is speaking may matter more than the words themselves. And that's illustrated in Nihal's last remark. To hear him talk of 'taking the piss' is neither here nor there. But when others use such language it can cause a real jolt.

Stewart Daker, who described himself as a 'collector for Christian Aid', wrote a thoughtful piece in *The Guardian*'s 'Face to Faith' slot during Christian Aid week. He mused on the reasons for hostility shown to collectors on the doorstep and included this sentence:

> I experienced too many doorstep transactions that revealed a public actively pissed off with religion.

Would he have written that a few years ago? I doubt it. Would a very senior politician have said what Margaret Beckett admitted to in an interview with *The Times* after she'd been promoted to foreign secretary? Again, I doubt it. She'd been asked for her reaction when Tony Blair told her she'd got the job. It was

> '. . . one word and four-lettered . . . beginning with the letter F . . .'

You might defend Mr Daker on the grounds that the rawness of his language expressed the strength of feeling he was reporting having found. But it may be that he thought using such street language would be more likely to get the readers' attention. As for Mrs Beckett, she's a plain-speaking woman at the best of times and, no doubt, was just being honest. But language has consequences.

The philosopher Mary Warnock believes there is a direct link between what she calls 'polite language' and polite behaviour. We are a rude society, she says, because we are not taught from childhood that there is a polite language 'different from the language we use with our mates'. A study by the think-tank Demos looked at the attitude of employers towards the current crop of graduates. One of the things they worried most about was their inability to deal politely with customers.

I learned a lot about language from Nihal though I doubt I'll be making much use of it on Radio 4. But I still can't draw a dinosaur.

CHAPTER EIGHT

Don't Diss It

At the end of the 2005 election campaign, Tony and Cherie Blair gave an interview to the *Sun*. The paper – as is the way with these things – boasted that this was a genuine exclusive: the first time the Blairs had given a joint interview. And, as is also the way with these things, it was mostly pretty dull. The fun came later when the Blairs posed in the garden at Number Ten for pictures – or, as the paper put it, 'cuddled under the cherry blossom'.

The photographer was one Arthur Edwards, a legend in his own darkroom, who is known as much for his cheeky-chappie relationship with his subjects as he is for his pictures. Arthur had asked Mr Blair – who'd just been voted (eat your heart out, Clement Attlee) Torso of the Week – to take off his tie for the pictures. Here is how the conversation between the three progressed:

TB: I'm not doing anything cheesy, Arthur, so don't ask.

CB: Oh, come on, Tony, strip off. Let's see that fit body we've been talking about.

TB: You can keep your hands to yourself, Cherie!

AE: So how fit are you, Tony?

CB: Very!

AE: What, five times a night?

TB: At least. I can do it more depending how I feel.

AE: Are you up to it?

CB: He always is!

TB: Right that's enough – interview over. And I'm not doing any kissing pictures! Come on, woman, time to cook my dinner!

As it happens, I was due to interview Mr Blair on the morning that that uplifting exchange appeared and it was the last thing I read before I nipped out of the studio for a pee. The nearest gents' is a small one: just two urinals. Standing at one – I didn't even know he was in the building – was the man himself. It is, I have to report, mildly off-putting trying to pee when you are standing next to the most powerful man in the land whom you are about (you hope) to reduce to jelly with the sheer brilliance of your interviewing. I wasn't having much success with the main purpose of my mission, so I tried some idle chitchat. Big mistake.

'I've just been reading about you,' I said.

'Oh, yeah . . . That stuff in the *Sun*, eh?'

The wise response was probably a smile. Instead I said: 'Yes . . . and if it was halfway true I'm surprised you can stand quite so close to the urinal.'

Big mistake, as I say. The first rule of conversation – engage brain before opening mouth – holds especially true when you are chatting with the Prime Minister in the gents' loo.

I was thinking of this when I came across the following remark of the great polymath, intellectual and all-round egghead, Jonathan Miller:

> 'There was a time in the early twentieth century when politicians and other figures of authority viewed the values of decency and sobriety as essential virtues of a civilised society. These values are certainly not cele-brated by our politicians and our media now.'

What interested me was not so much Miller's senti-ment as the almost throwaway phrase:

politicians and other figures of authority

I rather doubt that *any* of the politicians I know would see themselves primarily as 'figures of authority' or, indeed, whether many of them would even want to be seen as such. The idea might appeal to their vanity, but the hard political calculation would probably be that it would cost them votes. Politicians have stepped off their pedestals and want to come across as ordinary 'guys' – and, no, that's not sexist: nowadays women are guys too.

It has a lot to do with underpants. John Major was wont to tuck his shirt into his. Or at any rate that is what Alastair Campbell 'revealed'. I have no idea whether he did – any more than Mr Campbell did. But Mr Campbell was a journalist at the time – happy to spread the sort of nonsense for which he would later castigate 'irresponsible' journalists in his new career as spin doctor. The effect of his 'revelation' was, as Campbell intended, to make Mr Major look a bit of a nerd and it allowed the *Guardian*'s brilliant cartoonist Steve Bell to portray him for ever after in (and sometimes *as*) a pair of Y-fronts. And, of course, they happened to be the wrong sort of underpants. Conservative leaders can wear only boxers or briefs, as we discovered when the two contenders in the most recent leadership election happily discussed which they wore on *Woman's Hour*.

But never mind about politicians, what about the rest of Miller's phrase: 'other figures of authority'? Presumably the figures he had in mind from the past were judges, policemen, vicars and schoolmasters – even, perhaps, bus conductors, caretakers and park keepers. Not to mention parents and neighbours. My own recollection of being a small boy in what we would now call a working-class community is that we knew better than to challenge adults because they were almost all 'figures of authority'. And there would be no point in appealing to parents over a perceived (or real) injustice. In any conflict between child and adult, the adult's authority was invariably upheld. As a result, we accepted the notion of adult authority.

I wonder what would happen if you filled a room with such a varied group of adults today and asked who saw themselves as a 'figure of authority'. No doubt judges would put up their hands immediately: without authority they're done for. But among the rest I reckon there would be a great deal of uncomfortable shuffling in seats and muttering that the word 'authority' was one they didn't feel very comfortable with. Not that they would *want* to lack authority, you understand, but it's not really how they would choose to be regarded.

The adult neighbours, I suspect, would walk out. They might excuse themselves by saying that the only safe common rule in communities now, is that everyone should mind their own business.

Parents would say that authority gets in the way of being friends with your children.

Vicars would plead that hardly anyone was listening to them anyway and there'd be even fewer if they posed as figures of authority.

The police would perhaps say that if you came down too hard on the authority thing you'd end up with unnecessary confrontation.

And schoolmasters would point out that they don't exist any more: they're now teachers – except for some of the younger ones who are encouraged to think of themselves as 'facilitators', enabling the child to learn rather than telling them what they should know.

In short, the word 'authority' is one for which we seem to have less and less use.

You can almost see the word disappearing before our eyes. The world of public administration was once stuffed with 'Authorities' of one sort or another. Now they are much more likely to be called Agencies, Regulators, Commissions, Directorates and the like. The body now running public transport in London was originally going to be called the London Transport Authority but became Transport for London instead. Privatisation turned the Thames Water Authority into Thames Water, and the British Airports Authority into BAA – though that may change now that the Spanish own it. Occasionally a new authority is set up – to organise the London Olympics, for instance – but it tends to be the exception and, in this particular case, doesn't quite have the ring of, well, authority about it. It's called the Olympic Delivery Authority. How exactly do you 'deliver' the Olympics? An image of milk floats comes to mind.

Nor do we speak much of someone being 'an authority' on something or other. We talk instead of 'experts'. But there's a difference. Experts are specialists. We think of them as knowing everything there could possibly be to know about their narrow little fields but suspect they don't know much about anything else. Someone who was 'an authority' on something certainly knew what they needed to know about it but the phrase conveyed the sense that they could see it in the round – that they had something beyond mere expertise, perhaps even a whiff of wisdom.

There are various reasons why the word 'authority' is fading away. One is that it's a difficult quality to define. You know it when you see it but you can't put your finger on exactly what it is. Our culture is impatient with the indefinable. It hasn't time to be faffing around, musing about fuzzy qualities like authority. It prefers the explicit, the quantitative, things that can be expressed in a number.

Another problem for the word is that it invariably kept company with its close relation 'defer'. That's what you do to authority: you defer to it. You might argue with it, express your own point of view with passion and logic, but if you do not ultimately defer to authority it is gone. 'Deference' has already gone – and a good thing too if it means deferring to people because they are posher or grander or richer or more famous than we are.

My father was a highly skilled man – a french-polisher of the old school who would no more use a spray to apply his polish than Renoir would have done his painting by numbers – but quite clearly working class. He told me once how he'd arrived at a grand house to polish the piano. The servant who opened the front door ordered him to use the tradesmen's entrance. My father turned on his heel and told the flunkey that if he had to use the tradesmen's entrance his master could polish the bloody piano himself. They let him use the front door.

Deferring to authority is different. It is often essential in a well-ordered society. But first we have to respect it.

'Respect' is a word you might expect to have gone the same way as authority. But quite the contrary: you can't get away from it.

I appeared on *Da Ali G Show* at the height of its fame. A few days after the broadcast I was walking through a fairly dodgy area of London late at night wearing a suit, carrying a briefcase and trying, as you do, to appear inconspicuous. A group of young men on the opposite side of the street, wearing hoods and looking vaguely menacing, saw me, muttered something to each other, and crossed over. Oh, God, I thought, should I run? Too late. One of them raised his arm and I cowered.

'Respect, man! Ali G!' He slapped me lightly on the shoulder and off they went. It's funny how you don't get that response from your typical *Today* listener.

'Respect' is a word that's been kept alive on the street. There, it has spawned a new word for which we didn't really have an equivalent: 'diss'. Until it came along we made do with circumlocutions, such as 'He treated me with disrespect', but 'diss' is catching on. Indeed, I heard a senior, Oxbridge-educated civil servant using it in an entirely unaffected manner just the other day.

Politicians have caught on and are now talking about respect too. We have a 'respect' agenda –

central, at one time, to Mr Blair's final term in office. We even have a 'Respect' Party, even if some people aren't entirely clear what its supporters are meant to be respecting: the party's principles or its leader's willingness to prance around on *Big Brother* and lick cream off a fellow 'housemate'?

So does this all mean that we now have more not only of the word but also of what it represents? The evidence is, at best, confusing. The purpose of the government's antisocial behaviour orders (ASBOs) was partly to shame young delinquents into behaving more respectfully. But, according to a poll for MTV, a third of young men regard them as a badge of pride and the holder of an ASBO is accorded respect on the street. Which was not what was intended.

Perhaps this is what's going on here. Respect is rooted in self-respect. That, in turn, depends to a large extent on the sense of being useful, of feeling that you are contributing something of value. And that may be harder to do now. When I was a callow youth based in Liverpool as a reporter for the BBC, I interviewed a man who had been working on the building of Liverpool Cathedral all his life. That was forty years ago but I remember our conversation as though it were yesterday. The man was a stonemason and I asked him why he didn't get bored, laying one stone on another day after day, year in, year out. He seemed genuinely puzzled. 'But that's not what I'm doing,' he said. 'I'm building a magnificent cathedral.' His pride – his respect for this great task and his part in it – shone through.

Now things are very different. The sociologist Richard Sennett has captured the problem we face:

> In place of craftsmanship, modern culture advances an idea of meritocracy which celebrates potential ability rather than past achievement.

Sennett's worry is that when a society singles out only a few for recognition – as our celebrity-based culture tends to do – we end up with a 'scarcity of respect'. Somehow, being told that you are a 'valued customer' isn't the same thing. And if that's all we are it may be impossible to regenerate the sense of respect most of us crave. Consumerism has instead created a society characterised by the British doctor who writes under the pseudonym Theodore Dalrymple as 'egotism informed by a sense of entitlement'.

So it may be that much of this talk of 'respect' is no more than waving the word about. Literally, in some cases. From Iraq it has been reported that American military personnel based there are carrying around 'talking-point' cards with phrases such as

> We are a values-based, people-focused team that strives to uphold the dignity and respect of all.

There is a whiff of desperation about the exercise – as there is in this country. We are left chanting the word like a witch-doctor invoking the spirits, hoping something will materialise.

When a word loses its moorings it becomes available to be exploited. Picture this advertisement in glossy magazines: a full-page black and white photograph of a handsome young father, dressed casually in a white T-shirt, with fashionable stubble and kindly eyes. He's holding out in front of him his baby son. Across the bottom of the photograph in big red letters (inevitably in caring, non-aggressive lower-case) is the word 'respect'. Across his chest is this:

> I earn respect in my role as a trainer for young people; they ask me for advice, we exchange knowledge and discover who we are. It's really rewarding . . .

At the bottom left, in small letters, it says:

> Meet Romain Tissot Charlod, father of a newborn son . . .

So what exactly is going on here? This is a photograph of a man who trains apprentices. Right. They 'ask me for advice'. Fine. 'We exchange knowledge' . . . Hang on. You're the trainer, they're the trainees, so what sort of knowledge have they got that they can exchange with you?

'We discover who we are' . . . Excuse me? Are these some sort of religious self-discovery sessions you're holding? Do you sit around cross-legged? Is there incense? Would Sir Alan Sugar fit in?

And what's the main message? It seems to be that respect is really what matters most and we must make it central to our lives.

Well, all right, but what is the advertisement actually for? In the bottom right-hand corner, discreetly in red, is the single word 'Toyota'.

So the *real* message turns out to be that what we need to know when buying a car is that it has been built by a handsome young dad who's good to his trainees.

D'you think someone may be dissing us?

Like the word 'respect', 'trust' is much in vogue. But, unlike 'authority', it's being attached to things rather than removed from them. We once had local health authorities. Now we have primary care trusts and hospital trusts. It's probably meant to reassure us. Where the word 'authority' might have suggested bossiness, the word 'trust' implies reliability and security. The idea of 'trustees' smacks of people who are disinterested (in the correct meaning of the word) and possessed of that great quality, probity.

When the government decided to give state schools more independence it first referred to them as trust schools. That was what we were encouraged to think they would be called. But they were also talked about as foundation schools. 'Foundation' is another of those reassuring words: a house built on strong foundations will not fall and all that. But it was all a bit confusing. So I contacted the Department for Education and they sent me this email:

> What we are calling 'Trust' schools are
> Foundation schools with foundations. At present,
> the vast majority of Foundation schools do not
> have a foundation, and most of the schools that
> do have foundations are voluntary schools. The
> existing terminology is confusing – to simplify
> things we intend to use the term 'Trust school'
> and 'Trust'.

Well, that's cleared that up, then. I think.

But rather like 'respect', the more we use the word 'trust', the less of it there seems to be. I'm always hearing from doctors who say their patients don't trust them as they once did. That's partly down to the Internet. When my young niece discovered she had breast cancer she didn't simply accept the diagnosis from her doctor, go away and do as she was told. She hammered away at every website she could find, tracked down every bit of information about every treatment and its effects, contacted dozens of other women with breast cancer through various support groups and ended up so well informed she could probably have qualified as a consultant in her own right.

Many doctors say this can only be a good thing. They would much prefer to treat people who have a genuine, intelligent understanding of what's wrong with them and who know how much or how little can be done to get them well again. But not everyone is as sensible as my niece and there are plenty of patients who are hopelessly misled or even conned by some quack 'expert' who destroys their trust in their own doctor.

Inevitably – in every case – it changes the relationship between doctor and patient. The good thing is that doctors can no longer play God. The bad thing is that we may not believe them when we should.

The philosopher Onora O'Neill said in her 2002 Reith Lectures, *A Question of Trust*, that we face not so much a crisis of trust as a crisis of suspicion. That is partly down to the new technologies. She thinks we should not be surprised that 'the technologies that spread information so easily are just as good at spreading misinformation'. With misinformation, of course, comes distrust.

It is because trust, at the most fundamental level, has disappeared that most of us are terrified of smiling at a child in the park or helping her if she seems to be in trouble. My local playground has big notices warning adults to stay out unless they have a child with them. Children are warned not to trust adults and adults don't trust other adults not to label them weirdos if they show the slightest interest in their kids. Teachers aren't trusted to slap a bit of sun cream on a child or even stick a plaster on a cut without a sworn affidavit from the parents, a lie-detector test and the Archbishop of Canterbury or the Pope vouching personally for them.

I'm sorry to inflict this image on you but as I type this I am sitting in a pair of shorts in front of an open window. London has just had its hottest June weekend on record. It's stifling. But (and I bet you know exactly where this is going) on my desk is a newspaper article about the primary school where the children have been told they must wear their long-sleeved jumpers all the time – unless their parents sign a 'consent form'. It's worth quoting the school's headmistress, Joan Lawlan, at some length:

> "We remind parents all the time and as the sun becomes more noticeable [sic] we remind them again. We add names to the list as parents give their consent. They must do that, it's very important. When we go out for PE the children must wear jumpers if they haven't got parental consent . . . When we were young certainly it wasn't an issue, but with the media attention now, it's very necessary. We know about the dangers and we are very vigilant."

I know these stories are now more common than fleas on a camel. Parents must sign 'consent forms' for just about everything except breathing. That's fair enough if the school wants to take the child up the Amazon in a dugout canoe hunting for crocodiles, but it's obviously absurd for parents to have to give written permission for their child's photo to appear on a noticeboard. So why is it required? It's to do with the fear of paedophiles. 'Hysteria' is a more accurate word. Of course everything possible must be done to thwart them. That is so obvious it hardly needs stating. But does anyone really think these daft new measures will make the blindest bit of difference? Even the Health and Safety Executive itself is worried about what it calls the 'cotton wool' culture.

There is something ineffably sad about this – and I'm not just referring to the poor little blighters sweating in the sun who might, in a more sensible age, have had a dollop of sun cream slapped on them by a concerned teacher. They'll survive. It's the head-mistress who has my sympathy. We may be tempted to scoff at her for not using a bit of common sense, but it's the line about 'media attention' that gets to me. The poor woman is so worried about what the media will do to her if one of her little charges gets red arms and the mother complains that she finds herself plastered all over the papers for doing what she thinks is the right thing to protect them. Media hysteria is a big factor in all this and let's not pretend it's only the red-top tabloids that do it. In place of trust such hysteria breeds paranoia.

Samuel Johnson said, 'It is happier to be sometimes cheated than not to trust.' Our trouble is we seem to find it harder to take the risk of being cheated. So, to make sure we won't be, we've started to depend on another word: accountability. Now there is a word with a solid – indeed a solemn – pedigree. The Good Book itself tells us that on the Day of Judgement everyone shall be required to give an account of themselves. Or, to use the language of modern accountability, they must be ready with data on their deliverables.

'Deliverables' is a word much loved in business management-speak. It means a target that can be specifically and explicitly identified as capable of being delivered, so that once it has been, everyone can pat themselves on the back and say how wonderfully successful they are. Trebles all round.

It is in the nature of deliverables that they deal only in quantities that can be measured and given a number. That's fine for most businesses because what they handle can usually easily be quantified. Accountability is quite close to accountancy. Businesses are used to reducing everything to numbers: profits, turnover, share prices. The bottom line is what counts. It's interesting, incidentally, how the phrase 'bottom line' is catching on in ordinary speech and is taken to mean 'the only thing that in the end need concern us'.

It's a bit more tricky with deliverables when the thing being handled cannot be counted easily. There's no problem in measuring the number of cars sold last month and the profit made on them, but what about measuring, say, the care of patients? Before accountability came along in this numbers-and-targets way the question didn't really arise. In our private lives we made do with a rather fuzzy, qualitative assessment of whether Granny was getting the sort of care she needed or the GP was up to scratch. We might not have been able to measure it, but we knew if the service was good and we knew if it was bad. More or less. We still do. It's called judgement. But increasingly that's not how the public sector feels able to do things.

It provides services which, by their very nature, have a strong element of the unquantifiable, the immeasurable. What, for example, defines a good education? Not an easy question but whatever it is, you cannot reduce good education to deliverables. Yet over the years politicians have painted themselves into a corner in which they are desperate to show they can do just that. They need 'deliverables' to be accountable to the voters. Hence something called the 'audit explosion': the setting of myriad quantitative targets throughout the public services and the ceaseless paper chase to check whether or not they are being met. The result is that the old qualitative way of assessing things has rather fallen by the way.

A friend was shocked by how far this had gone when he turned up to a parents' meeting. He asked the history teacher how his daughter was getting on and he was presented very professionally with a spreadsheet and a graph. *This* was where she was now and, on the assumption that her performance levels stayed constant, *this* was the trajectory she'd be following so *this* was the Key Stage Three grade that could be expected.

Yes, but did she show an interest in history? Did she seem to enjoy it? Did she contribute much in class? My friend didn't get very far with these questions. His attention was constantly redirected towards the graph and the performance indicators. Deliverability in action.

It happens in the private sector too. I talked to the headmaster of a small prep school in London a few days after it had had its annual inspection. The inspector wanted him to list, in descending order of importance, his ambitions for the school and its achievements. The first thing he wrote was 'A happy school'. The inspector was puzzled. What about exam results and reading standards and assessments of coursework? As it happens, they were all pretty good, but the headmaster had put them much lower down the list. Why? 'Because,' he told me, 'if the children aren't happy they're not learning.' The problem for the inspector was: how do you measure happiness?

Numbers are beguiling because they are simple to use. It's easier to glance at the star rating the critic has given the film than to plough through his five hundred words on why and make your own judgement. We seem to have a touching faith in numbers – or perhaps it's more like fear of them.

I forced myself (in the interests of research, you

understand) to watch one of those hideous pro-grammes in which a bossy woman goes round to some ordinary person's house and tells her how to live her life. It seems to me to be a form of sado-masochism – the soft-core version that's allowed on before the watershed.

This one was about household cleanliness and the bossy woman had a gizmo that measured hidden grime. The housewife (the Scottish chapter of the Women's Institute is debating banning the word even as I write) had, of course, made it spotless for the cameras. When the gizmo was pointed at the tell-tale area round the fridge, it confirmed that all was fine. But when it was directed at the wooden chopping board, the dial started whirring, smoke poured out of its innards and the numbers hysterically announced that there were at least a gazillion lethal bugs lurking there, ready to strike down the entire neighbourhood.

The poor woman looked utterly devastated. Whether she survived the horror I have no way of knowing. What I wanted her to do was seize the gizmo from the bossy woman's hands, smash it over her bossy head and scream: 'The figures mean nothing! I've been using wooden chopping boards all my life and so has my mother and her mother before her and if there really are a billion bugs on mine I couldn't give tuppence. I *like* bugs – now bugger off!'

As it happens, I once shared a kitchen with Gordon Ramsay. I was competing with him to see who could cook the best lamb curry. Yes, he won, but only just and only because I didn't buy my own chillies. (These chefs are *very* competitive. Almost as bad as journalists.) Anyway, we fell to talking about chopping boards. For the television show he has to use those horrible plasticky things ('elf'n'safety, of course). Guess what he'd prefer. Yet the statistics show the plastic ones are 'safer' and even Mr F-word himself is cowed by the figures.

The point about figures is meant to be that you can't argue with them. But, of course, you can. Cecil B. DeMille once said to a group of critics: 'Gentlemen, those are my principles. And if you don't like 'em . . . I've got others.' There are always other figures too.

Interviews with Gordon Brown have not been the most fun-packed moments of my life. P. G. Wodehouse once wrote that it is seldom difficult to distinguish between a ray of sunshine and a Scotsman with a grievance. He might have substituted 'a Scottish Chancellor with a statistic'. The point is that Mr Brown always has more statistics and they invariably serve his cause. Of course they do. That's why he selects them. Like any other politician in the history of politics – or any businessman for that matter – he chooses the statistics that make his point. There is another way of doing it: George Bush's way. He dealt with Trevor McDonald when he presented him with a set of figures to prove how America is polluting the environment by saying:

'Well, I just beg to differ with every figure you've got!'

When the need to demonstrate accountability is seen to be vital in building trust, 'deliverables' matter. But if the figures are, at best, capable of misleading and, at worse, meaningless, we have a problem. Here's how Onora O'Neill puts it:

> Perhaps the culture of accountability that we are relentlessly building for ourselves actually damages trust rather than supporting it.

So how can we re-establish the reality of trust and respect and authority? Fortunately this is a book about language and not about how to put the world to rights. I leave that bit to you.

CHAPTER NINE

Talk Like an Amateur

Beneath the crest of the BBC are these words: 'Nation shall speak peace unto nation.' It is hard to think of a more stirring sentiment. If the BBC makes even a tiny contribution to this noble aim, then its existence has been justified. Yet there are times when I wonder if it should be replaced with this:

One either meets or one works.

Those are the words of one of the world's most successful management gurus, Peter Drucker. I grant you that, as a motto, it doesn't have the same ring to it, let alone the power to change the course of history in quite the same way. But what a thought – an organisation like the BBC committed to doing away with meetings.

Of course it will never happen. World peace is far more likely – a cinch by comparison. The people who would have to decide to end meetings in favour of work are the very people who spend their lives attending them. Take away the meetings and you take away the reason for their existence.

In all big organisations some people succeed by being very clever; some by being very lucky; some by working very hard; and some by being very good at meetings. They know when to keep their mouths shut and when to offer a judicious opinion. They can spot the way a meeting is going and support the boss's view even before he has offered it. It is a genuine talent.

When *Today* comes off the air and the team troops into the editor's office for the 'inquest', I stand in the doorway with one foot in and one foot out. I never sit down. Childish, I know, but it means I can claim that I never go to meetings. What *is* the point of them? If a couple of people get together they can reach a decision. If a dozen people get together they cannot.

People go to meetings either to guard their own backs or because they have nothing better to do. I once knew a very smart businessman who ran the European division of one of the world's biggest IT companies. Year after year its profits and turnover increased sharply. Then sales started to fall and kept falling. So he announced that during the final quarter of the year all meetings would be cancelled – except those with customers. The graph began to rise again. Many of those middle-management types who had spent their time talking to each other were talking to the customers instead.

So, Drucker is right. One either meets or one works. One reason to prefer working is to dodge the language that's spoken in meetings. There's not much point in nation speaking peace unto nation unless they can understand what each other is saying. When I hear some of my colleagues I frequently don't. Try this for size:

> The transition to an on demand digital environment requires a shift to an asset centric approach to media asset management, capturing meta data at the outset of the assets lifecycle. This in turn enables greater movement and sharing of audio & visual material across the BBC to deliver increased exploitation of assets.

Let me not suggest for a moment that the BBC is any worse than any other large bureaucratic organisation. They all have their equivalent of bosses who 'engender the buy-in of content creators', whatever that might mean. One qualification for being a manager is that you learn this silly language. Perhaps it doesn't matter very much if they spout it at each other behind corporate walls and leave the rest of us out of it.

In this sense the gobbledegook virus is a bit like bird flu. One does not like to think of chickens or geese getting it but that's not half as frightening as the prospect that it might jump the species barrier and infect humans too. Well, I have bad news. The gobbledegook virus has mutated and is infecting the wider population. Here is a random selection of phrases:

- Forward-looking companies invest in functional organisational capability.

- A vision of expanding contestability in the delivery of offender services.
- The consultants recommend parallel management matrix approaches.
- The process of external challenge needs to be robust . . . which is why we'll be looking at cross-cutting questions of resources.
- The transport secretary will have to reflect on whether the government could do more to leverage its relations with the security industry.
- Only geeks stuck in the 90s still go for compatible reciprocal concepts.
- I assure you that my prethinking will be rational.
- When we have looked at targets we've done the gap analysis so we know the bridges that we have to cross.

Some of those were generated by the Plain English Campaign gobbledegook computer. Most were spoken by politicians. If you can't tell which, then, as astronauts occasionally report to Mission Control, we have a problem. But it's worse than that. It is one thing for the virus to jump the species barrier between business and politics. Worryingly, it has crossed into the world of real people too. It has done it by first infecting the public services.

The general consensus among politicians is that what the public services need is not only an injection of market forces but much greater involvement of charities, or 'the voluntary sector', as they are now known. The government has something called the 'Civil Renewal Scheme' to bring them on board and most charities are more than willing to get stuck in.

The trouble is that volunteers (who tend to speak English) come up against bureaucrats (who tend not to). The chairman of a local Princess Royal Trust for Carers in Hampshire wrote to me some time ago in exasperation at his experience. His committee had been sent a six-page document called 'Government Support for the Voluntary and Community Sector' outlining how it was hoped that charities could help improve public services – or rather (infection having already set in) 'driving forward programmes to improve' them. The document included the sentence:

> The Infrastructure Strategy will join up with capacity building recommendations from linked pieces of work, to form an overarching strategy for implementing the capacity building and infrastructure proposals from the Cross Cutting Review.

As the chairman put it to me:

> 'None of our committee was other than perplexed by this foggy English.'

Even within charities the virus is spreading. That's because the term 'voluntary sector' is itself a bit misleading. It brings to mind draughty church halls with ladies of a certain age manning bring-and-buy stalls to raise funds to stop the spire falling down. It evokes the tin-rattlers who stand in the cold all Saturday morning outside M&S smiling gratefully as they stick a badge on you in exchange for a quid – not that they are allowed any longer to do the sticking themselves lest they be accused as assault.

But that's only half the story – perhaps less than half. The voluntary sector is, to a large degree, not voluntary at all. It's made up of full-time professionals paid to do a job. It could hardly be otherwise, given the tasks the charities have to perform.

As a result they're gradually changing the name to the 'Third Sector'. Its motto is supposed to distinguish it from the other two: 'Not-for-profit and mission-driven'. I think if I were in the private sector I might want to protest that I'd be out of business if I didn't make a profit. And if I were a public-sector worker I might want to say I felt pretty 'mission-driven' too. But as everyone is in a partnership, there are probably no hard feelings.

With the new professionalism of the Third Sector, though, comes the virus. Nick Aldridge, the director of strategy and communications at the Association of Chief Executives of Voluntary Organisations, has written a pamphlet trumpeting the potential for the Third Sector in public-service reform. It includes sentences such as:

Third Sector providers are able to work across government silos, joining up funding streams and policies.

Anyone who can join up funding streams and silos in the same sentence will go far.

But back down among the volunteers it all seems rather baffling. A woman who works in a charity in south London told me it was a case of Indians and Chiefs. The Indians are the people doing what they have to do for the people they're helping; the Chiefs are the professionals in the office filling in the forms. They speak different languages. She told me:

> 'A lot of their language bears no relevance at all to what happens on the ground.'

Older volunteers, she says, are 'totally exasperated' not just with the alien language but with what it represents: the transformation of their charity from the kitchen table and the rattling tin to the computer terminal and the huge mailshots. They don't believe it helps them provide a better service.

She knows they have no alternative but to burble on about 'empowerment' and 'excellence' and 'best practice'. They have to speak this stuff, she says, if they have any chance of raising the money they need because much of that money comes from the government.

The rules require them, for instance, to demonstrate that they pursue what are called 'SMART aims'. And what are they? They are Specific, Measurable, Achievable, Realistic and Time-related. How bureaucrats love their acronyms. Now, that's fine except that 'achievable' and 'realistic' amount to the same thing. So couldn't the criteria be reduced to four? But then it would be SMAT aims or SMRT aims, neither of which has quite the same ring. So SMART aims it has to be, which means that form-fillers everywhere struggle to find something to write in the 'Realistic' box that hasn't already been included in 'Achievable'.

There are other ways of doing good works than joining a charity: become a school governor, perhaps. But don't imagine you will be spared language abuse if you do. A friend of mine (I'll call her Jane: she'd rather not be identified for reasons that will become clear) signed up to be a parent governor when her daughter joined a north London comprehensive school. If she had been expecting to stroll along to a few meetings and keep a benign eye on things she was in for a shock.

In one respect she was hugely impressed. The business of being a governor was taken extremely seriously. She found herself immersed in a highly organised Governor Development Training Programme. She was inundated with documents and scrupulously ploughed her way through them. It struck her that even when the language of bureaucracy was not jargon-laden and obscure, it often had nothing to say beyond the blindingly obvious. And then it said it again. And again.

For instance, she was given a 36-page glossy brochure about the borough's 'Healthy School Scheme'. She read a section, spaciously presented in bullet-point form, on how being part of the scheme helped schools. Then there was a section on how it helped pupils. Then one on what teachers who'd been part of the scheme had said about it. Then one on what the results of being part of the scheme would be. By now she felt she'd pretty much got the picture.

And then she turned to page nine. I am a bit reluctant to inflict this on you but it really won't do just to give you a flavour. You need to read the whole thing to appreciate what poor Jane and her fellow governors had to suffer. Here goes:

What Is a Healthy School?

- A Healthy School is a place which is an enjoyable and safe learning environment in which pupils can achieve their full potential and gain knowledge, understanding and skills to be able to lead healthy lives.
- A Healthy School is an inclusive school which values the diversity of its community and has policies and practices that reflect this.
- A Healthy School involves parents and the community in the promotion and maintenance of health.
- A Healthy School considers the health and well-being of staff as well as pupils.

- A Healthy School is active in promoting positive health and minimising potential health risks.
- A Healthy School will have a range of healthy school activities that reinforce the learning from the classroom.
- A Healthy School will be concerned about these topics: the environment and safety, healthy eating and physical activity, drug, alcohol and tobacco education, sex and relationship education, PSHE and citizenship, pupil support and consultation, staff health and welfare, teaching, leaving and achievement, partnerships and leadership and management.
- A Healthy School will also be concerned about its health-related policies, how health education is co-ordinated and planned, how pupils are involved and consulted, teaching and learning, how parents, governors, staff and the local community are involved, and how pupils' achievements are recognised.

In short

- **A Healthy School is an effective school.**

By now Jane was beginning to wonder if she had made the right choice. Instead of becoming a school governor perhaps she should have enlisted in the special forces and learned to abseil down buildings, crash through windows and force every bureaucrat in sight to eat nothing but crisps and drink nothing but

Coke while simultaneously smoking and engaging in unprotected sex. It's funny what too much of this sort of stuff can do to you. But she's tough, is Jane, and she kept reading.

Still to come were sections called 'Key Features of a Healthy School', 'What Is the Healthy School Scheme in Camden and Islington?', 'Principles of the Scheme', 'Aims of the Scheme', 'Achieving the Aims', 'Key Elements of the Scheme (details in Section Two)' . . . and this would take her only to page twelve.

There was also a schedule of meetings for new governors to attend. There were sixteen to choose from. Some seemed straightforward enough: 'Induction Part 1: Your Strategic Role'. Others she passed over rather quickly (she felt she was an expert by now on 'The Islington Healthy School Programme'). This one caught her attention:

Know your PANDA and your SMIF (Enjoy & Achieve)

You may think that enjoying a smif (let alone a panda) is not the sort of thing that should be happening in our schools. But, of course, the ADD (the Acronym Design Department) has been in action again.

'Enjoy and Achieve' is a reference to the government's 'Every Child Matters' initiative. Let's pause there a moment. Can you imagine any government launching an 'Only a Few Children Matter' initiative? Quite. A bureaucrat was then set the task of defining

'Every Child Matters: Outcomes'. These were: be healthy; stay safe; enjoy and achieve; make a positive contribution; and achieve economic well-being.

So, this meeting was all about category three. But what have enjoying and achieving got to do with pandas and smifs? Well, a panda (pay attention at the back, please) is the new Performance and Assessment Report and a smif is the School Management Information File.

There's also, in case you're interested, a SEF, the Self-Evaluation Form. So new governors might have been invited to a meeting to know their PANDA, their SMIF *and* their SEF. But one can have too much of a good thing – even enjoyment.

I'll spare you all the bullet points about pandas and smifs except one. It said that attending this meeting would

- Enable governors to consider and formulate some of the questions they might ask about the school's performance in their role as 'critical friend'.

Jane, an intelligent woman, wondered why she was deemed incapable of formulating the odd question without the aid of all this mumbo-jumbo. Might it be that only certain sorts of question would be welcome, even from a 'critical friend'?

She decided to forgo the pleasures of pandas and smifs but she did attend a meeting of new governors run by the outside professionals now responsible for her daughter's school. It was a bit like going to a revivalist meeting conducted in management-speak. It was full of boosterish language to do with how passionate everyone was about everything. But it was also peppered with words and phrases such as 'consultation', 'collaboration', 'partnership', 'addressing outcomes', 'sharpening up the action plan' and 'developing a proposal about your engagement'.

When, finally, she had had enough she blurted out that she hadn't the faintest idea what they were all talking about but it most certainly wasn't what *she* wanted to talk about. Her equally bemused fellow novitiates, who'd seemed a bit cowed by it all until then, joined in to back her up. The panda people seemed genuinely shocked, she told me. No one, it seemed, had ever complained that they were incomprehensible. It couldn't be true.

Jane's account made it sound rather like an episode of *Doctor Who* in which aliens, looking just like humans, are engaged in a dastardly conspiracy to seize real human beings, infect them with a virus and convert them into members of the conquering alien race. For aliens, read professionals; for humans, read amateur volunteers; for the virus, read language.

Deprive people of their own language and make them use another and they're a long way to being held captive. My friend came away from that first meeting with the impression (fair or unfair, she couldn't yet tell) that what those who ran the school were hoping for from their new governors wasn't so much an independent guiding voice but people who would simply nod through what they wanted.

The takeover of our affairs by pseudo-management language is no more than a reflection of our changing attitude to the amateur and the professional. It has turned a hundred and eighty degrees.

Not so very long ago the amateur was considered superior to the professional. That was partly for bad reasons, based on class (the players and the 'gentlemen'), and partly for good reasons. There was the sense that the amateur was more committed, was playing the game or running the race for the love of it. The origin of the word is *amo* and even people like me who gave up Latin after two years know what that means. Using the language of management-speak, it was the amateur, not the professional, who was 'passionate'.

Now 'amateur' is a term of abuse. An 'amateurish job' is one that has not been done properly; a 'professional job' can't be improved upon. We all want to be thought of as professional. That's fair enough in most ways. I wouldn't be terribly keen on having open-heart surgery from a keen amateur. But we badly need the enthusiastic amateur in so many ways. Even the panda people talk of schools needing 'critical friends'.

But friendship is not a profession and friends, by their nature, are not professionals. They are different from the doctors, psychiatrists, counsellors, probation officers and other professionals who advise us on how to live our lives. Our friends are amateurs and usually they give the best advice.

Volunteers are the friends of communities. If they are not left to speak their own language, if they are not allowed to remain amateurs but are coerced into being the hangers-on of professionals, they will disappear back into their private worlds.

There is the occasional ray of sunshine breaking through this gloomy sky. Read this and rejoice:

> 'My priority is to ensure that players feel more amateur than professional. Thirty to forty years ago, the effort was the other way. Now there is so much professionalism we have to revert to urging players to like the game, to love it, do it with joy.'

Bet you can't guess who said that. It was Big Phil, otherwise known as Felipe Scolari, regarded as one of the best football coaches in the world. He ran the Brazilian side when it last won the World Cup. And it was his Portuguese side that knocked England out of it in 2006. How extraordinary that a man at the very top of the most 'professional' game in the world, where players routinely earn £100,000 a week and are bought and sold for the price of a small country, should have come to such a conclusion. Mr Scolari was offered the job of managing the England side but he turned it down.

The brilliant sports writer Simon Barnes once argued that football matters too much. The person who can 'free himself from the straitjacket of professional concern and play the damn ball without thinking about it too hard' wins the real prize. And if he can do so with joy, so much the better.

Football, I'm afraid, bores me to death but even I can see the beauty in the game when it is played for the love of it as well as for the spoils of victory. A society run only by professionals is not one I much fancy belonging to. Apart from anything else, it would be one endless meeting.

CHAPTER TEN
Gissa Job

Does anyone tell the truth, the whole truth and nothing but the truth when they apply for jobs? I doubt it – but it may be that I'm simply trying to lessen my own sense of guilt. I'm ashamed to say that I tricked my first editor into giving me a job. I pretended that I had been a leading light at my school. To use the words of a former cabinet secretary, I was being at the very least economical with the truth.

The editor invited me to tell him what I'd been best at. Difficult, I said, given such a list of things to choose from, but it had probably been my prowess as a long-distance runner. The editor was mightily impressed: 'Just what's needed in a young reporter – plenty of stamina. You're hired.' Or words to that effect.

The truth is that I had made absolutely no impact on my school or it on me. I left at fifteen and when I went to see the headmaster for a reference it was perfectly clear that he hadn't the faintest idea who I was. He obviously knew what I had not done. I had not made it into the school rugby team, or the cricket team, or the hockey, tennis, swimming or falling-off-a-log teams. I hadn't even made it into the B teams. If I had been remotely athletic – or even particularly brainy – he would have known. He was one of those headmasters who were interested only in what we now call the 'gifted and talented' kids.

I suppose I shouldn't hold it against him, but I do. Some years later, after I'd achieved what passes for a modicum of fame in my strange trade, the school asked me back to speak at the annual prizegiving. I said I'd be delighted, then told them what I would say. The invitation was hastily withdrawn.

But all of that hung on my becoming a trainee reporter for the *Penarth Times*. My claim to be a long-distance runner was true as far as it went – but that was not very far. Every Wednesday afternoon in winter we were forced by our sadistic PE teacher to put on our daps (plimsolls, if you weren't born in South Wales, and trainers, if you were born any time after 1980) and run a few miles through the cold, wet streets of Cardiff. I think it was meant to be good for our characters.

Naturally the teacher didn't come with us: he was a sadist, not a masochist. I usually managed to grab my bike as we left the school, cycle round the course, stop for a gossip with someone, and get back reasonably swiftly without breaking too much of a sweat, but it was enough for that vital entry on my so-called CV and enough to impress my first editor. That was nearly half a century ago and, mercifully, I have had to apply for only three jobs since then. The rest

I managed to stumble into. For that, I am truly grateful.

It's not that there seems to be any shortage of jobs – not if you scan the media or public-sector appointments pages of *The Guardian*. The problem often is trying to work out what on earth they are. Employers seem to need some very odd creatures. Try these for size:

- A Common Assessment Framework Co-ordinator (Merton)
- A new Head of Innovation Clusters (Birmingham)
- Diversity Officers, decibel legacy (The Arts Council)

Haringey advertised, quite simply, for a 'Hints Visitor' and South Tyneside had a job going in 'Decriminalised Parking Enforcement Services'. I'd love to know what criminalised parking services are but it's probably best not to ask.

Beware, though, of guessing what a job ad might mean. A keen astronomer might think Staffordshire's post of 'Sub-Regional Observatory Co-ordinator' would be ideal for him – but not after he'd read the description. It's actually about 'providing cross-cutting information for Stoke-on-Trent and Staffordshire Strategic Partnership'. Obvious when you think about it, I suppose. Age Concern's need for a 'Signpost Agency Manager' presumably has nothing to do with all those road signs that clutter our streets. And I very much doubt that Swindon's 'Domestic Violence Co-ordinator' does exactly what their job title suggests. On the other hand, we do have a body called the National Domestic Violence Steering Group, so you never know.

Sometimes the language is so bizarre you may not progress even as far as getting the wrong end of the stick. As I write, the Camelot Foundation is advertising for tenders from bodies who might run this:

A Virtual Centre of Excellence on Self-Harm

I'm sure it will do a valuable job, but there must be a better way of phrasing it. Do the people who come up with these titles ever step back and imagine what such a group of words might appear to mean to those who are not already engrossed in the project? And does 'virtual' mean the salaries will be virtual too?

Organisations get into this sort of absurdity because they become so used to their own management jargon they forget that other people speak English. Kent Police, for example, advertised for a new 'Head of Project 2015'. The blurb said:

You will work in a highly politicised environment with significant exposure to external stakeholders.

I suspect they might be referring to the public. It did not say whether surgical masks would be provided.

Reading job advertisements is a bit like looking for somewhere to live and traipsing around one house after another. After a while you start to see the appeal of a camp site. With houses, it's other people's wallpaper, carpets and kitchen units that make your spirits sink. With job ads it's the language.

The people who place the ads seem to appreciate this and try to offset the effect by throwing in a few uplifting adjectives. But somehow it always seems a bit self-defeating. Thus, for example, this ad placed by head-hunters for the job of managing director of an unnamed company somewhere in the Thames Valley:

> This is a business critical role with an important division of a highly respected leading global organisation. With a strong reputation for creatively meeting market demand through an array of high value services, our client is at an exciting stage in its growth cycle.

When you get to 'creatively' you begin to realise this is just language wearily being wheeled in to do a job; by the time you reach 'exciting' you want to run away and do something that is genuinely exciting and creative, such as rearranging your sock drawer.

Once words like 'exciting' lose their oomph, substitutes have to be found. The current favourite is 'passionate'. The London Development Agency advertised for a public liaison officer. The ad explained how the successful candidate would be expected to do the job:

> When we talk to stakeholders, our message is simple – we're passionate about improving London for the benefit of people living and working here.

Oh, come on! I'll grant the LDA may be keen, enthusiastic and committed, but 'passionate'? I don't want to be indelicate but passion is something that rather comes and goes. It's not something you can keep up all the time, so to speak. If I were a 'stakeholder' (perhaps I am, for all I know) and some young public liaison officer from the LDA kept coming over all passionate with me I think I'd run a mile.

The hype raises the stakes for what is expected of those poor souls looking for the jobs. Foxtons, for example – with the gloriously absurd slogan 'People Not Property' – advertised not simply for a Sales Coordinator but for an 'Energetic Sales Coordinator'. The blurb pitched it even higher:

> Foxtons is recruiting for a Superstar to support a busy Sales Director at our stunning HQ.

This puzzled me because, in a separate ad entitled (for some reason that escapes me) 'Extreme' and with a photo of a young man in a wetsuit surfing the waves, it said:

> Foxtons have revolutionised the property market in London by constant innovation in every area of our business to exceed our client's expectations.

You'd have thought if they had only one client they could take things a bit more easily in servicing him. Or maybe it's *because* there's only one client they so desperately need an energetic superstar. Seems a bit mean to pay only £25,000, though.

The effect of all this hype is not just to inflate the job but to set the tone in which applicants feel obliged to inflate themselves. Bizarrely, some job ads go as far as writing the script you must perform in the interview. An organisation called Creative Sheffield ('a mould-breaking, UK-first initiative aimed at creating one integrated lead organisation . . .') advertised for a chief executive. The text of the ad included this:

> Your undoubted passion for cities, coupled with a proven track record in managing complex regeneration agendas and economic master planning, will enable you to influence key movers and shakers . . .

Hang on. Isn't the point of an interview to discover whether candidates really do have an 'undoubted passion for cities'? Set the script like this and every candidate will feel compelled to show up proving they're on urban Viagra. Another paragraph began:

> Bringing a sense of urgency and a passion for change, you will rationalise and integrate the functions of . . .

If you were preparing for the interview after reading this ad, what strategy would you come up with? Turn up five minutes early, barge into the interview room and immediately set about rearranging the furniture before telling the marketing director to 'integrate' with the sales director or clear off?

This sort of language is not only silly but self-defeating. It forces candidates into a narrow role. The older, more formal way of advertising jobs didn't fall into this trap. The ads essentially did two things: they defined the job and tried to deter futile applications by including a sentence that read something like

> The successful candidate will have a degree and at least three years' experience in . . .

What they did not do was talk about 'you'. It meant that interviews could be more genuine opportunities for candidates to present themselves as they really were and – who knows? – some might even offer qualities whose value hadn't occurred to those trying to fill the post.

There is something odd, perhaps even slightly chilling, about the tendency to define 'you' so specifically that you have no option but to try to conform to the portrait they have already painted of you. Aren't they interested in who you *might* be? It's as if they're inviting you to hide yourself rather than present yourself. They see the interview as a performance – but one that is acted to their script rather than yours.

After the job comes the appraisal. You might think you've been doing reasonably well and so might your boss – but what about everyone else? A new phrase has entered the world of work: 'the three-sixty'. To give it the full title it's the '360-degree appraisal'. It means that everyone watches everyone else and then writes down what they think of them – anonymously, of course. You and your boss sit down and chew over what they've said about you. This can include anything under the sun – not just your professional competence, but your personal habits too. I can see some benefits in this. If *Today* presenters were ever 'three-sixtied' I would definitely report Jim for his habit of eating his polystyrene coffee cups. No doubt he thinks they're tastier than the coffee, but still . . .

Some people like it. One very senior civil servant told me she had volunteered (correction: 'proactively sought') a three-sixty when she changed departments because she had no other way of discovering how well she was doing. She argued that there were perfectly good reasons why all her colleagues – junior as well as senior – should have a say in how she did her job. Others hate it. One middle-aged curmudgeon told me he pores over his appraisal when it's handed to him, submits it to detailed textual analysis, works out precisely who must have said what about him, then devotes his life to plotting revenge. There is talk in some dark corners of the education world of allowing pupils to 'appraise' their teachers. There may be more lunatic ideas around, but I'm hard-pressed to think of one right now.

It's not so much the process that gets me as the language. Orwell would have loved it. Substitute 'surveillance' for 'appraisal' and at once Big Brother is watching you – only now your colleagues are the spies, keeping tabs on you from every angle. It was Orwell's case that once we buy into the language of something hitherto alien to us we are well on the way to accepting it. Here the alien notion in the phrase is that we should be under surveillance all the time and pounced upon if we transgress. Beyond work, we seem already to have accepted that with scarcely a murmur. There are more CCTV cameras in this country than just about anywhere else on earth and no one seems to mind.

Here's another phrase that has entered the world of work in recent years: 'work–life balance'. It's something we must all have, it seems. If we don't have one (and it must be the *right* one) we are doomed. Politicians keep talking about it and it's very hard to get through a day's newspapers without someone, somewhere, boasting that they've got theirs just right or they're desperately worried because they haven't. It is one of those verbal formulas whose terms we tend to take for granted. But if you think about it, it's quite odd.

If I had asked the mason working on Liverpool Cathedral back in the 1960s what he felt about his work–life balance, he probably wouldn't have known what I was talking about. He might have said that his work–*leisure* balance wasn't quite as he'd like it and that he'd prefer to spend a bit more time with his family. But as for his life, his work was so much a part of it that it made no sense to talk of it as something separate.

But he was a craftsman: the cathedral, or at least his small part of it, was his life's work. Most people don't have something solid they can point to in the same way. I don't suppose William Morris ever used the expression but back in the middle of the nineteenth century he saw that the retreat of craftsmanship in the face of industrialisation would mean that, for many people, work would be likely henceforth to cut against the grain of life rather than be naturally integrated with it. So did Karl Marx. The origins of our fashionable phrase could be said to go back that far.

A hundred and fifty years later some people are still lucky enough to feel their work goes with the grain of their lives. I'm one of them. My work–leisure balance is appalling but that's my choice and I make it because work and life for me are so intertwined. I keep getting called a workaholic but the truth is I'm one of those lucky people whose work is 'naturally integrated' with his life. I usually have three or four jobs on the go at the same time and can no more imagine retiring than I can retraining as a catwalk model. Work is as much a part of my life as leisure. I love building Bionicles (if you don't have a small boy to do it with it's best not to ask) or walking in the hills, but I also love asking questions of a politician on the radio or a *Mastermind* contender on television. The difference, by the way, is that one lot actually *wants* to answer the questions. I neither 'live to work' nor 'work to live'.

But if you look at some of the phrases used about our working lives it's not hard to see why for many people work and life are opposites rather than complements.

Have you, for example, 'reinvented yourself' recently? This is the buzz phrase for the new economy. We all know that the era of a job-for-life has disappeared. My parents could imagine nothing better for their children than a job in an office (ideally a bank) with a steady income and a pension at the end of it. In my own industry I know young graduates today who would willingly crawl over broken glass and set fire to their underpants if it gave them the chance of a three-month contract as a junior researcher. It is not uncommon for them to work for film-production companies for nothing. They might get their bus fares paid – if they're lucky. It is not that competitive in most other industries, but the idea of the carriage clock at the end of forty years' faithful service has gone the way of spats.

So we must now 'reinvent' ourselves. Some people will welcome the chance to vary their work; others will regret it. But as for the language, it is an extraordinary phrase to use about human beings.

Psychologists tell us that to make sense of life we must construct for ourselves a 'sustaining life narrative' that gives it meaning. I'm not quite sure how we do that if we need to keep reinventing ourselves. It might have been necessary for Lord Lucan when he went on the run or *Big Brother* 'celebs' when we've all forgotten why we ever knew them, but it's pretty tricky for normal folk. Think of it this way: how would you follow *Hamlet* if the hero popped up as Macbeth in the second act and King Lear in the third? Not easy. 'Reinvent' neatly captures the divorce between life and work that many people feel.

And here's another of the new buzz phrases to do with work that shows how alien it can be to life: 'de-layering'. Management consultants love it. It means breaking down the old hierarchical structures of companies in which everyone knew their place – and that's no bad thing. I had a friend who worked in middle management for Tesco when they had more grades of staff than cans of beans. The rule was that if someone was two grades above you, you called them 'Mr' (or, very rarely, Miss) no matter what your personal relationship. But at least there was some sense of belonging and of mutual loyalty. Now, when companies are de-layered they get rid of all those middle layers and there's just the powerful centre and you. It makes sense in some organisations – but it leaves people feeling exposed if they're not at the centre.

There's a lovely old cartoon that shows a boss with

his feet on his large desk and a sweating underling standing before him. 'Make it easy for me, Jim,' he says. 'You don't know how terrible it makes me feel to tell you you're fired.'

No, it wasn't meant to be Alan Sugar. In today's de-layered company you probably won't even get that face-to-face meeting with the heartless swine: possibly just an email telling you to collect your P45. As George Soros, the billionaire financier and philanthropist, put it: 'Transactions have replaced relationships in people's dealings with one another.' So perhaps it's not so strange that to many people work and life now seem opposed to each other.

In the midst of all this fresh-faced language of de-layering, reinventing and work – life balance a very old word has made a reappearance: 'happiness'. Even economists, who tend to prefer such dreary phrases as 'utility maximisation', have been heard using it. Politicians make speeches about it. Academics produce studies on it.

What's exercising them is the discovery that not only has becoming richer failed to make us happier but it seems to have contributed to our being less happy. And they've come up with an expression to describe the phenomenon: the 'hedonic treadmill'.

I had never heard the word 'hedonic' and assumed they had made it up. But there it is in the dictionary: 'hedonic (1656): of or pertaining to pleasure'.

The hedonic treadmill theorists claim that, in the never-ending process of working to earn to spend, we are now getting less satisfaction from the spending and more grief from the working. Wordsworth put it both more poetically and more clearly two hundred years ago:

Getting and spending, we lay waste our powers.

And he spotted that long before the consumer society got going. I doubt if he received much junk mail through the door of Dove Cottage offering to lend him a couple of grand to blow on a holiday.

The nineteenth-century American novelist Herman Melville warned us, too, about the seductive temptations of the hedonic treadmill when he wrote (with rather more style):

Seeking to conquer a larger liberty, man but extends the empire of necessity.

The fact is that sensible people have always known that money cannot buy happiness – even though it does make you a little more comfortable in your misery. The publisher Felix Dennis, who became so rich he wrote a book about it, says that although money does not make you happy it does improve your sex life.

But what gives all this recent talk of happiness and treadmills a bit more significance is that the predicament we've started to gripe about is no less than the utopia that the Western world has been striving to reach for the last five hundred years or so. We single-mindedly set about getting richer. We have succeeded. We in the world's richest countries have now achieved a level of material well-being (to say nothing of being able to live as long and healthily as we do) that would have seemed to our forebears like the realisation of utopia.

It was a utopia forecast by the economist John Maynard Keynes:

> There will come a time when we've solved the economic problems – at which point we shall be faced with the permanent problems of mankind: how to live wisely, agreeably and well.

How much richer do we have to get before we realise we've arrived? Yet having reached this utopia we seem to have discovered it's not what it was cracked up to be. We've now not only started talking about hedonic treadmills but we've begun to find a use for a word that means the very opposite of utopia: 'dystopia'.

That's a word that was previously so unused that the *Oxford English Dictionary* didn't even include it until 1972. Now it's become quite common to see modern life being talked of as a dystopia. And the need for the word seems not unconnected to treadmills because as another economist, John Kenneth Galbraith, remarked when talking about utopias, there are many versions of the good life 'but the treadmill isn't one of them.'

Still, that's probably not something to bring up at your next job interview.

CHAPTER ELEVEN

Back to School

An old friend from my years in South Africa had come for supper and I cracked open the last bottle of a case of wine I'd brought back with me thirty years ago. It had not improved with age but we drank it anyway – then started on a different case to take the taste away. So when my five-year-old crawled into my bed at about three in the morning my parenting skills (when did that ghastly phrase enter the vocabulary?) were sadly lacking.

'Dad,' he said urgently, 'we need to talk.'

I've noticed with clever little boys that they almost never say 'want': it's 'need'. I suppose they pick it up from us: 'You really need to brush your teeth/go to bed/eat some more of that broccoli.'

'What about?'

'Is Africa a bigger country than England?'

I sensed that this was not going to be easy but I tried to explain about continents and countries and said that, yes, Africa was very big indeed and much bigger than England. There was a short pause.

'Why did Jesus allow that?'

God help me. Perhaps if I'd done a philosophy

degree I might have tried explaining what a 'category mistake' is. Perhaps I could have gone down the theological route and dealt with Jesus as part of the Trinity or explained the Big Bang or the continental drift. But a combination of too much bad wine and too little sleep meant I was barely able to form a sentence. 'Ask your teacher' was the best I could manage. I'm not proud of it. Indeed, I'm ashamed. But there it is. Anyway, the teacher must have put the idea into his head in the first place.

Teaching is not easy and many teachers say it is made no easier by the demands of politicians and bureaucrats. It has never been so difficult to recruit head teachers. It was once the case that a school advertising for a new head struggled to choose from the mass of applicants. Now qualified teachers tell me they are almost afraid to walk past the school in case they are dragged in and tied to the head's empty chair.

They offer a number of reasons for this apparent lack of ambition. One is that schools have become exam factories and all that matters is that they manage more passes at better grades this year than last. The children are trained in the skill of passing tests, rather than getting the broadest possible education. The other complaint (not unrelated) is that teachers and heads are required to be managers and bureaucrats, endlessly filling in forms and meeting targets.

We parents may sympathise with them but there is often a touch of hypocrisy in our approach. Many of us speak with forked tongue. Yes, of course we want our little sprog to get a good, rounded education – but if he doesn't get the exam results we expected or do as well as his best friend we'll damn well want to know the reason why. And may the saints preserve the brave teacher who tells the pushy parent she's sorry that little Samantha hasn't done awfully well in her exams, but her talents lie in other directions.

The language of the teaching world gives some interesting pointers as to what is going on:

> The school has a policy of 'Eye Shine' days, whereby teaching staff are encouraged to, on occasion, suspend the curriculum and do 'a one-off' to excite and stimulate the children.

This comes from what is known in the business as a SEF – a 'Self-Evaluation Form'. It was filled in by a London primary school. It was in the box where schools are invited to note anything that might interest the Ofsted inspectors when they make their next visit.

On the face of it there's something rather charming about an 'Eye Shine' day. It suggests paintings of big yellow suns stuck on the school walls, their rays spreading out in all directions and a smiling face in the middle. But it suggests something else too.

It suggests that there is something special about an 'Eye Shine' day: that it is the exception rather than the rule. The implication is that only on special, earmarked days will the children's eyes shine with the joy of being taught at that school. Presumably the rest of the time, when the children are on the treadmill of the curriculum, plodding their way towards the next set of exams, their eyes are glazed over rather than shining brightly. Why else call the 'one-off' days 'Eye Shine' days?

No doubt many teachers will get cross about this and tell me it's not like that in their schools. I hope they're right. But there have been big changes in primary education since my elder children started school more than thirty years ago. We have had the national curriculum, more and more testing, school league tables and all the other apparatus for 'raising standards'.

Tests have become what would now be called the main 'driver' of everything. They matter to schools because they are the measure of how the school is doing in competition with others. They matter to pupils, of course, and they matter to parents because they will help determine which school their children get into next term. It creates pressures all round. That helps explain why a young teacher in a reception class said her four year-olds no longer had a sand table or water-play area: either might distract them from the serious business of hitting their targets.

One primary-school teacher told me how she has tried to create an oasis from all this by setting up a little poetry magazine to which pupils could contribute if they wished. There would be no marks, no points; it would be for the fun of it. It had been going for a while in a relaxed sort of way when an anxious middle-class mother came up to her at a parents' evening and said it was really important that her son had a poem published in the magazine. Well, fine, said the teacher, if he wrote something that she and the other children thought should go into it, it would. But that wasn't good enough for the pushy mum. It was *vital* he should have a poem in the magazine because it was 'needed for his CV'.

An eight-year-old with a CV? That's enough to dull the eyes of the brightest.

It seems a consensus is growing that all this may have gone a bit too far. The Qualifications and Curriculum Authority has admitted that 'the assessment load is huge' and announced that it wants to cut the number of tests in schools by a third. And a pamphlet, *The Shape of Things to Come*, published by the Department for Education and Skills Innovation Unit acknowledges the problem. Its author, the consultant and innovation guru Charles Leadbeater, writes:

> Many children feel education is something done to them, a period they must endure. This leads many to disengage from education or, worse, disrupt it.

The basic idea is that we need to replace the old 'send-and-receive' model of education, in which a teacher stands in front of a class and sends out teaching material the pupils are supposed to receive. Children don't so much need to learn 'stuff' as to 'learn how to learn'. Then they can do it for themselves. The solution is what is being called 'personalised learning'.

For this to happen (so the argument goes) the old organisational model of a school, in which pupils sit in classes following rigid timetables of fifty-minute lessons, needs breaking up a bit. Because children have varying ways of getting the hang of things, schools should be less rigid. Children should be free to explore ways of learning in small groups. Older children should help younger ones. There should be more one-to-one tuition and so on.

All of this amounts to 'personalised learning'. Leadbeater quotes Derek Wise, the head teacher of Cramlington comprehensive school in the north-east.

> Each lesson they come to should be organised into a cycle of activities – show the point of the lesson, connect it to things the children have already learned, introduce new information, allow the children to process that through an activity and demonstrate they have ingested it, debrief.

I confess, it sounds to me a bit like reinventing the wheel. That description is not a million miles from what competent teachers did with us when I was at school. In fact, getting children to learn how to learn is what good teachers have been trying to do since

Socrates. But perhaps the wheel really does need reinventing, and if schools have the resources to do more personalised learning, good luck to them.

What's new here, though, is the language in which this is couched and especially what it seems to say about our attitude to children. In the foreword to the pamphlet Valerie Hannon, the director of the Innovation Unit, writes:

> I hope *The Shape of Things to Come* provides a constructive challenge to policy makers and practitioners alike, helping to frame how we can begin to fulfil all of our aspirations for a personalised learning offer for every student.

If teachers still used old-fashioned blackboards that phrase 'personalised learning offer' would be the equivalent of a fingernail scratching down one. It's more than just a dreary piece of business-speak. It implies that a child is a client or a customer, the figure to whom the 'offer' is made. It becomes even more extraordinary when it's combined with what Leadbeater writes at the beginning of his pamphlet:

> . . . the ultimate goal of personalised learning [is] to encourage children to see themselves as co-investors with the state in their own education.

Come again? The ultimate goal is that children should *see themselves* as co-investors with the state? I reckon if a child came up to me and said she saw herself as a co-investor with the state in her own education I'd have serious worries about her welfare. I'd start wondering whether management consultants had begun to form sinister sects, grabbing kids in playgrounds and indoctrinating them in business-speak. Get 'em by seven and they're yours for life, as the Jesuits put it.

You may think this is just a silly piece of drafting and not worth fussing about. What he clearly meant was that the ultimate goal is to motivate children so that they are as keen to get themselves a good education as the state that's paying for it. Amen to that. But the language suggests a reluctance to talk about children as children. And that is because we couch so much of what we say in the jargon of business and markets.

All business relationships are between adults. So, to borrow the language of business, the 'stakeholders' come across as adults even when they are children. A child cannot be a 'co-investor' without in some sense ceasing to be a child. If we see people only as either consumers or producers or investors – and the lexicon of business allows no other categories – we lose the means to talk about children in ways that recognise they are children. *The Shape of Things to Come* seems peopled by children who are eight going on thirty-eight.

Leadbeater seems so imbued with this language that he even parrots a version of the oldest management cliché in the book – so whiskery that even managers groan when it's trotted out at business conferences by bosses wanting to say nice things about their staff:

> Our education system's biggest untapped resource is the children themselves.

I know what he's getting at but it's hard not to wince at the notion of children as an 'untapped resource'.

The shift away from language that allows us to talk about children as children is pervasive. Here, for example, is Eddie O'Hara, the Labour MP for Knowsley South, speaking in the House of Commons:

> 'At the end of this month, all Knowsley secondary schools will be closed and replaced with eight learning centres.'

This followed the abolition of the title 'director of education' and its replacement with 'director of children's services'. O'Hara said this was all part of the 'systemic, inclusive, corporate and holistic agenda' in Knowsley. The term 'learning centre' apparently reflects this.

I'm not at all sure that I know what that list of adjectives means but the words 'education' and 'school' are missing. They have been replaced: we now have 'children's services' and 'learning centres'. This is more than just another of those rebranding exercises. Changing something's name changes how we think of it.

The word 'school' has been used to describe many things but its basic association is with children. School is what everyone does between the ages of five and sixteen. It's a large part of what childhood means. 'Learning centre' does not have that association. Anyone can attend a learning centre. If children start going to learning centres something characteristic of childhood is taken away from them.

That may be deliberate. Some adults have always thought it would be a good thing if children were not treated so much as children but more as young adults. I think that's wrong. There is a difference between treating a child with condescension and attributing to him a maturity he cannot, by definition, possess.

But there is an even more important distinction that comes with the language. You go to a learning centre but you belong to a school. The difference matters because a school is (or should be) more than a learning centre, and what children learn there is more than their lessons. They learn what it is to belong to something beyond their own family – an institution with a life of its own that does not exist solely to serve their individual needs. A vital part of growing up is learning that the world is not just an extension of yourself but that you are part of something bigger.

To use a word we fret a lot about these days, a school really is a community. 'Learning centre' does not have that ring. It has much more in common with 'health centre' and 'leisure centre' – places that are there to serve you, not places that also make some demands on you.

Did I say 'demands'? Hmm. Dangerous word, that. Might, like, turn off the kids . . . know wha' I mean? Better not risk doin' their 'eads in, innit? I mean, wot we gonna do if they fink *Twelfth Night* is a pain in the jacksie to study? Obvious, innit? We do a revised version with lots of silly pictures and jokes and use language even the dopiest squid-for-brains can understand.

That appears to be more or less what Coordination Group Publications believes. 'Pain in the jacksie' is their phrase, not mine. It's on their website. And they happen to be publishers of educational texts widely used by schoolchildren from Key Stage One to A Level. 'Squid-for-brains' is what Macduff calls Macbeth in their helpful guide. Martin Samuel of *The Times* treated his readers to a flavour of how it works. You may remember that Shakespeare wrote these lines:

ROMEO: If I profane with my unworthiest hand
　　　This holy shrine, the gentle sin is this:
　　　My lips, two blushing pilgrims, ready stand
　　　To smooth that rough touch with a tender kiss.
JULIET: Good pilgrim, you do wrong your hand too much,

> Which mannerly devotion shows in this;
> For saints have hands that pilgrims' hands do touch
> And palm to palm is holy palmers' kiss.

ROMEO: Have not saints lips, and holy palmers too?

JULIET: Ay, pilgrim, lips that they must use in prayer.

ROMEO: O, then, dear saint, let lips do what hands do;
> They pray, grant thou, lest faith turn to despair.

JULIET: Saints do not move, though grant for prayers' sake.

ROMEO: Then move not while my prayer's effect I take.

This, according to the guide, is what he meant to say:

GIRL: What are you thinking about?

BOY: Oh, just moons and spoons, in June.

GIRL: Wow. Give us a snog, then.

Let's try a few lines spoken by Lady Macbeth:

> Was the hope drunk
> Wherein you dressed yourself? hath it slept since?
> And wakes it now, to look so green and pale
> At what it did so freely?

Guide version:

> Cowardy custard!

Or a few lines from Macbeth himself:

> Is this a dagger which I see before me,
> The handle toward my hand?

Guide version:

Oooh! Would you look at that.

Or:

> Thou canst not say, I did it; never shake
> Thy gory locks at me.

Which becomes:

Bloomin nora its (*sic*) Banquo's ghost.

Yes, I know it sounds as if I'm making it up, but you can check it for yourself.

It's not that we shouldn't try to make the greatest writer in English come alive for children. That is what good teachers do. But the point of studying Shakespeare is to engage with his thought, his language and his poetry because that will enhance students' lives. This sort of thing, as Professor Alan Smithers put it with what must have been enormous self-restraint, 'seems to be circumventing that engagement'.

Yet it works. It produces, in the language of commerce, satisfied customers. Last year more than 126,000 copies of the guides were sold to schools and in shops. No doubt it made Shakespeare – in the word that has come to epitomise all that is good in education and culture – 'accessible'. It delivers the service. Why bother to struggle with the complexity of Shakespeare's language when you can glance at the silly drawings and bowdlerised version and get the gist of it? The value of Shakespeare is in the beauty of his language. But 'value' means something else in the language of commerce.

The relentless onward march of technology is beginning to have a real effect on the language. Take spelling. The Oxford English Corpus – a massive database compiled by Oxford Dictionaries – monitors just about everything that's written these days from websites to blogs and newspapers to books. It has found a huge rise in spelling errors, most of which stem from the Internet. Some have changed the meaning of phrases that have been around for a very long time. A few examples:

> strait-laced: 'straight-laced'
> just desserts: 'just deserts'
> sleight of hand: 'slight of hand'
> fazed by: 'phased by'

Much more serious is the effect IT is having on the way our children learn. The neurobiologist Baroness Greenfield is worried about the distinction between those of us educated in the twentieth century and our children and grandchildren educated in the twenty-first. We had books; they have computers. What we get from books and the written word, she says, is guidance. The controlling mind of the author steers us through a lot of disparate material, giving us a conceptual framework of understanding. We may not agree with it, but we can read other books and gradually our own framework builds up.

One might argue that this is the basis of education – education as we know it. It is the building-up of a personalised conceptual framework, where we can relate incoming information to what we know already. We can place an isolated fact in a context that gives it significance. Traditional education has enabled us, if you like, to turn information into knowledge.

Children educated in this century are spending on average six and a half hours a day using electronic media – often 'multi-tasking' with two different devices on the go at once. Increasingly, the electronic media rely more on the icon than the word. But most of all, she points out, the quick-fire, fast-moving nature of much electronic media militates against building up a personalised conceptual framework.

Imagine that you are sitting in front of a multimedia presentation where you are unable, because you have not had the experience of many different intellectual journeys, to evaluate what is flashing up on the screen. The most immediate reaction instead would be to place a premium on the most obvious feature, the immediate sensory content – we could call it the 'yuk' or 'wow' factor. You would be having an experience rather than learning. Here, sounds and sights of a fast-paced, fast-moving, multimedia presentation would displace any time for reflection or any idiosyncratic or imaginative connections that we might make as we turn the pages, then stare at the wall to reflect.

I've talked to Lady Greenfield about this. She worries about a link between the time children sit in front of screens and the number of 'hyperactive' children being treated with drugs. If I were a half-awake fifteen-year-old, seeing adults first over-stimulate me, then sedate me with drugs, I'd feel I was being cheated.

It all comes back to shining eyes. At five, children's eyes are shining most of the time, even at those moments when they suspect Jesus may have cheated them about Africa. What we should want, once they have been taken off into the world of education, is for their eyes to go on shining perfectly naturally.

CHAPTER TWELVE

Bad Smells

The language of politics is changing. A generation ago the following sentence, which appeared in the *Financial Times* recently, would have been incomprehensible.

> Andrew Cooper, director of pollster Populus, said the Tories' opposition to ID cards and glorification was about 'brand positioning'.

Substitute 'selling biscuits' for the political stuff in that sentence and there would have been no problem understanding it. Selling biscuits or cars or trainers is all about brand and always has been. But it's new in politics. I'm not suggesting there was ever a golden age when politicians used only elegant argument to persuade the voters of their strongly held convictions. If you believe that, reading a little Trollope will set you right. What's new is the way in which politicians themselves acknowledge the reality.

It is no longer offensive or even controversial to acknowledge that politics is now essentially about marketing. About selling a product. About packaging a party and its leader so that both look appealing. It's about creating and positioning a brand in such a way that consumers/voters want to buy/vote for it.

So the advertising gurus have been in the driving seat – or, at least, doing the map-reading. One of the most famous and successful of them, Maurice Saatchi, was the first to have a really big success with a political client, Margaret Thatcher. Remember 'Labour isn't working'? But now he has announced that advertising in general is dead. That has implications for politics and for the role that language plays in it.

Among the reasons he gives for the death of advertising is that the digital age has bred something called CPA: 'continuous partial attention'. Lady Greenfield would know exactly what he's talking about. It seems that our minds – and especially the minds of our children, who represent the future – are distracted in ways they have never been before.

We are simultaneously distracted by mobiles and iPods, the television in the corner, the Gameboy we're playing and the magazine we're reading. So distracted that we can no longer concentrate long enough even on the slogans of political advertising – never mind detailed argument. Lord Saatchi comes to an intriguing conclusion:

> Each brand can own only one word. Each word can only be owned by one brand . . . The same applies to political parties or countries – Britain's Labour Party

won three elections with the word 'new'. America's one-word equity is 'freedom'.

As I write, the Conservative Party is in search of a new logo to replace the flaming torch ignited by Margaret Thatcher. We've had some harmless fun on *Today* inviting listeners to suggest a new one. What we should now do – all of us – is think of the one word with which our parties will be branded in future. Here are a few suggestions. You can decide for yourself which party deserves which:

- choice
- prosperity
- freedom
- peace
- contestability (no, I haven't the faintest idea either: ask Mr Blair)
- greed
- avarice
- sloth
- envy . . .

. . . whoops, sorry, getting carried away there.

But even the mighty Saatchi may be a little behind the times. It seems we may not need even that single word.

Now it may be all to do with smell. Fraser Nelson, the political editor of the *Spectator*, reports from inside the Conservative camp that the young Tory Turks have decided the real trick to winning power is simply to create an 'aroma'. Nelson quotes a senior policy maker as saying that 'vastly more important' than policies is the task of creating . . .

'. . . an aroma around the Conservatives so people naturally imagine our policies are the right ones'.

Stop sniggering! Smells are powerful. To this day I have only to smell old furniture polish and I am immediately transported back almost sixty years to my infants' school where we were allowed to rest our heads on our desk lids for a little snooze. Fresh bread takes me back to my grammar school, which was next to a bakery. The smell of freshly roasted bread and Chelsea buns (remember them?) was pure torture when it drifted through the classroom window. The smell of orange peel reminds me of the local flea-pit and Saturday mornings with Roy Rogers. So does the smell of stale pee . . . but we'd better stop it there. We all have our own set of smells and there will be plenty to analyse in the coming era of aroma politics.

Perhaps we shall have to develop a whole new vocabulary. Certain ministers will be fragrant; budgets piquant; policies complimented for their bouquet. But smells are also fleeting, will-o'-the-wisp, impossible to capture and pin down. Perfect, you might say, for what Robin Day called 'here-today-gone-tomorrow' politicians.

But until the time comes when I spend most of *Today* sniffing the air, there remains the task of dealing with the language politicians still use. Often, like a smell, it makes a big impact but is hard to pin down. For example, they frequently 'address the issue'. But what does that mean? It could be anything from considering setting up a working party to contemplate whether steps should be taken to forming a committee to recommend a policy review to come up with options for . . . well, to invading another country perhaps.

Or they borrow metaphors that sound solid in the original but evaporate into meaninglessness when they use them. So when things haven't gone quite as they should, they promise to 'raise their game'. If a crestfallen Andy Murray says it, you know he knows what he thinks he has to do. When a politician says it, it could mean anything. Or nothing.

One of the oddest of these phrases is 'redouble our effort'. Why not just 'double'? Does it mean they've already doubled their efforts once and that now we're in for a quadrupling? It can lead to delicious confusion. A Home Office minister used it at the time of the row over the releasing of foreign prisoners. A little later this headline appeared in *The Guardian*:

> Reid Warns That Foreign Prisoner Crisis Twice As
> Bad As Expected

I don't think that's what the minister had had in mind.

Some favourite phrases sound tough but are intended to dodge answering very specific questions.

One is 'send a signal'. It is particularly popular in the field of criminal justice. Let's imagine that a politician proposes that young thugs be strung up by their toes while their victims throw stones at them. In response to the odd sceptical question from someone like me, he might well brush aside the objection, dismissing me as another 'cynic' who just wants to 'do down' honest attempts to deal with the problems, and argue that in any case details aren't what matter. No, what really matters is to get the right message across to the thugs. Not to adopt the measure would 'send the wrong signal'.

A relatively new phrase in the repertoire is 'direction of travel'. It's another device for dodging specific detail and talking instead about the 'broad picture'. I spotted it first when the government was trying to get its Education Bill through the House of Commons and was encountering some pretty determined opposition from its own back benches. It became quite difficult at times to know exactly what the rebels didn't like, especially after the government had made some concessions to them. We were told that it was the 'direction of travel' that upset them. In other words, the rebels could concede the government's good intentions but feared this particular direction of travel might be paved with them.

But we must not be too harsh on politicians. Sometimes when their language appears designed to dodge rather than address an issue it's only because they are representing us: it's we who are doing the dodging and they are taking their lead from us. Here's a much-used phrase:

We need to strike a sensible balance on this.

Most of the time that is precisely what they try to do – strike a sensible balance between the conflicting demands of tax and public spending, say, or an unfettered market and regulation. The problem arises when there is no 'sensible balance' to be struck, when the issue is so black and white that compromise is not an option.

Global warming is a good example. All the leaders of our main political parties agree that it is the most serious issue facing the world today – even bigger, says Mr Blair, than international terrorism. The experts agree that air travel is making things worse and is the fastest-growing source of carbon emissions. The number of flights from Britain will double over the next twenty years. But it is a very brave politician who will say we should fly less. They know we like our cheap flights so they say we must 'strike a sensible balance'. How exactly do you strike a balance between a cheap weekend in Prague and the future of the planet?

The 'sensible balance' lies not in dealing with the problem but in minimising a potential loss of votes. It's we, the voters, who abuse the phrase 'sensible balance'. The politicians merely utter it.

You may detect an unexpected sympathy for politicians in these remarks. And why not? It's much easier to interrogate them than to be one. We ask an awful lot of politicians – though, admittedly, they tend to encourage us.

When the government announced that it wanted to create 'dignity nurses' in every hospital to make sure that elderly patients were treated with proper courtesy (shouldn't every nurse do that?) a news bulletin said:

Ministers Want Patients To Complain

Do we really need ministers to get us to do something we're perfectly able and willing to do without them? I imagine the patient being approached by a concerned official as she lies in her hospital bed: 'Oh, you *must* complain, dear. We mustn't let that nice Mrs Hewitt down, must we?'

This assumption that politicians should be responsible for just about everything can lead them into some bizarre use of language. Here's a health minister talking on *Today* about child obesity:

'It's a hugely complex issue because it's not just about food, it's about exercise.'

Umm . . . True . . . It *is* about both food and exercise. But does that really make it hugely complex? The minister was responding to a report on obesity by no fewer than three watchdog bodies: the National Audit Office, the Audit Commission and the Healthcare Commission. It emerged that responsibility for reaching the government's targets was in turn shared between three government departments: the Department of Health, the Department for Education and Skills and the Department for Culture, Media and Sport. Beginning to get complex, isn't it? And now read what the boss of one of these bodies had to say:

> 'The challenge is that there has to be leadership from the government departments. That then has to flow down to the regional level so that at the regional level there is some clarity over funding and who's doing what. But that isn't sufficient. It then has to go right down to the local level. And at the local level what we're talking about is teachers working *with* children, *with* parents and also local authorities coming together as well to provide – because this isn't just a question of what children eat, it's also a question of ensuring that they get exercise . . . so it's quite a challenge for people locally to provide that advice . . . At the moment there isn't enough guidance for people really locally about what they can do that's effective. So what we need is more guidance and more examples about best practice to enthuse people locally.'

The blindingly obvious is made to seem 'hugely complex' simply because such a clutter of bureaucracy is created to deal with it. And that is because we demand politicians be responsible for so much.

Politicians have come up with a word to explain the nature of this complexity. The problems, we are told, are 'systemic'. This is a useful word for politicians. Charles Clarke used it about problems at the Home Office. It's useful precisely because it is not one we use in everyday language. It makes it sound as though it's something only experts would understand. But the real beauty of it is that it says it is the 'system' that is at fault – rather than any individual or specific group of people. If it were 'systematic' the fault would clearly lie with humans – and heads would have to roll.

One of the words that has most altered its meaning is 'debate'. I once lost a sweepstake over how many times a trade-union leader I was due to interview would use the word 'debate' (i.e. 'What we need is a debate about this') during a twenty-minute interview. I bet four. The winner guessed seven. The trade-union leader said it twelve times. I have some sympathy for him because I think he meant it. Mostly when politicians use the word they don't mean it at all. Or they mean something else.

It's a perfect illustration of the difference between textbook politics and modern marketing politics. In the textbooks, debates really do take place and decisions flow from them. In modern politics, decisions are often taken before the debate. It is rare for them to affect the decisions. Instead, when politicians say they want a debate it usually means they want to 'send a signal' rather than receive one. The signal is that they realise the rest of us may be het up about something so they want to be seen to be onside. But they don't want to lose control of an issue lest it affects (sorry 'impacts') their marketing strategy.

There is a helpful lexicon of phrases on which politicians may draw when they want to close down debate. Here's a sample:

- 'in the real world' (if you disagree with me you're bonkers)
- 'let's not play the blame game' (we only play this when it's the other lot who've cocked up)
- 'move on' (yes, we cocked it up last time but, hey, who's counting?)
- 'we mustn't hark back' (because we want to move on)

Bill Clinton, widely regarded as the most brilliant politician of his generation, liked to say: 'Never look back. *Never!*' What a luxury that would be in the world outside politics.

When politicians have to deal with crises of world-changing dimensions they sometimes resort to language that seems designed at worst to confuse and at best to distract. I wrote in *Lost for Words* about the curious word 'rendition', which was just creeping into our vocabulary. It transformed itself subsequently into 'extraordinary rendition', even though the activity it described was unchanged: moving prisoners from one country to another where the rules of interrogation were somewhat less restricting.

When Condoleezza Rice, the American Secretary of State, was asked about Iran she said:

'The invasion of Iran is not on the menu at this time.'

What a strange, homely phrase to use in such a context. When members of the Bush administration started having doubts about Guantánamo Bay because of the world's reaction, some began to regret ever having set it up. They referred to it as an 'impulse buy'.

Guantánamo Bay has provided some of the best examples of how wayward and adrift from reality political language can become. Sandra Hodgkinson, the deputy director of the Office of War Crimes Issues (itself a wonderful linguistic formulation) referred to 'the different care providers' at Guantánamo Bay. 'I was just down at Guantánamo Bay yesterday,' she chirruped, as though she were talking about having dropped in on her local nursery school. Rear Admiral Harry Harris, the camp commander, had his own, perhaps more characteristic way of talking about the same issue:

'We aggressively look for ways to build on the "safe and humane care and custody" mission . . .'

When people talk about the same thing in such radically different language, what is revealed is how differently they see the world – or, even more, how differently their jobs *make* them see it. This became strikingly obvious when three prisoners committed suicide in June 2006. Rear Admiral Harris described it as

'an act of asymmetrical warfare waged against us'.

I suppose he was seeing it as a military man. But another American official, Colleen Graffy, Deputy Assistant Secretary of State for Public Diplomacy, said:

'Taking their own lives was not necessary but it certainly is a good PR move.'

Ms Graffy had her knuckles rapped for that, but if you see the world only in PR terms you will end up assuming everyone else does too. It brought to mind the legendary remark of Metternich, the Austrian diplomat famed for his devious approach, who assumed everything everyone else did was equally devious. He had been engaged in intricate negotiations for months with the Russian ambassador, who suddenly died. Metternich said: 'I wonder what he meant by that . . .'

Yet some progress with more simple, straightforward language is being made. When the American government realised that the phrase 'War on Terror' was not having the desired effect around the world they came up with a new name. It is now called 'The Long War'.

There's no fancy packaging in that. This is plain language in plain brown wrappers. The only alarming thing is this. How do they already know it's going to be long?

Sometimes the simplest language is the most chilling.

Last Words

Confucius said the first thing he would do if he ever became ruler was to rectify the names of things. In his book *Unspeak*, Steven Poole imagines asking him why. This was the answer:

> When the names for things are incorrect, speech does not sound reasonable; when speech does not sound reasonable, things are not done properly; when things are not done properly, the structure of society is harmed; when the structure of society is harmed, punishments do not fit the crimes; and when punishments do not fit the crimes, the people don't know what to do.

That's a pretty good explanation of why it is important to pay attention to language. It's not hard to drift into a Confucian dystopia – you might call it 'a confusion' – where words no longer mean what they are supposed to mean and nothing is what it is said to be.

Nearer our own times, William Cobbett recognised the same danger when he wrote:

> Those who write badly think badly . . . Confusedness in words can proceed from nothing but confusedness

in the thoughts which give rise to them. These things may be of trifling importance when the actors move in private life, but when the happiness of millions of men is at stake, they are of an importance not easily to be described.

Forcing ourselves to write properly forces us to think properly.

In the view of many people, much of public life now suffers from the condition Cobbett feared. The American writer Joe Klein says in *Politics Lost* that 'the expectation of spin [has] deafened the American public to the possibility of substance'. If people do not believe that words represent real things they cannot act as citizens. The United States, according to Klein, has become 'a democracy without citizenship'.

But it's not just as citizens that we need to keep an eye on words. Our society, which treats us so much as an audience to be entertained and as consumers to be led to market, often uses language as an anaesthetic. If verbal blandishments can encourage us to sit back and relax, we can be taken care of in more ways than one. And unless we're trained to be alert to the use of language we're likely to end up duped.

It is young people who are most vulnerable to the wiles of the marketing man. Peer-group pressure is more powerful at sixteen than it is at sixty. We crusties tend to glory in our defiance of fashion – which is, I suppose, itself a kind of conformity. But the young are not taught to use and understand language as older people were – one of the main reasons I wrote *Lost for Words* – and that makes them even more vulnerable. It is that much more difficult to think for yourself if you don't have the language. And a society in which people don't think for themselves is dangerous. 'A society of sheep begets a government of wolves' was how the philosopher Bertrand de Jouvenel described the consequence.

The link between our independence and the need to be watchful over language is captured perfectly at the beginning of Philip Roth's fine novel *I Married a Communist*. The narrator is looking back to his schooldays and to his inspirational teacher, Murray Ringold.

> 'In human society,' Mr Ringold taught us, 'thinking's the greatest transgression of all.'

So, approving of transgression, he set about teaching them how to think for themselves. Roth describes the experience like this:

> Mr Ringold knew very well that what boys like me needed to learn was not only how to express themselves with precision and acquire a more discerning response to words, but how to be rambunctious without being stupid, how not to be too well concealed or too well behaved, how to begin to release

the masculine intensities from the institutional rectitude that intimidated the bright kids the most.

'Expressing themselves with precision'; having 'a more discerning response to words'; learning how to be 'rambunctious without being stupid'. I'd be happy for Mr Ringold to teach my little boy.